FACET fb BOOKS

BIBLICAL SERIES—24

John Reumann, General Editor

Luke the Historian in Recent Study

by C. K. BARRETT

With a New, Select Bibliography

FORTRESS PRESS   PHILADELPHIA

First Published as the A. S. Peake Memorial Lecture No. 6
by the Epworth Press, London, 1961.

© 1961 by C. K. Barrett
Published 1970 by Fortress Press

PREFACE TO THE NEW EDITION, SELECT BIBLIOGRAPHY, AND THE

INTRODUCTION © 1970 BY FORTRESS PRESS

Library of Congress Catalog Card Number 75–81527

2259G69   Printed in U.S.A.   1-3057

Introduction

"An admirable survey of the subject," a book "which contains almost 'all we know and all we need to know' "—so the late C. S. C. Williams, of Oxford, and R. R. Williams, Bishop of Leicester, have described Professor C. K. Barrett's lecture on Luke-Acts to the Methodist Conference in England in 1961 (*Expository Times*, 73 [1961–62], p. 133; 80 [1968–69], p. 4). And while there is far more to know about Luke's two volumes, that "storm center in contemporary scholarship" (W. C. van Unnik), than these pages can recount, teachers who had found the book a handy introduction to the topic regretted very much the remaindering of the British edition. At their suggestion "Facet Books" is making available a new printing (correcting a few errors and updating a few references), adding a new bibliography on important publications 1960–69, with comments by Professor Barrett.

The author is Professor of Divinity at the University of Durham (cf. "Facet Books, Biblical Series," 6; *Biblical Problems and Biblical Preaching,* 1964, where his inaugural lecture on eschatology and an address on preaching are reprinted). His most recent books have been commentaries on the Pastoral Epistles (1963; see below, p. 63, note 65) and on 1 Corinthians ("Harper's/Black's New Testament Commentaries," 1968) and *Reading through Romans* (London: Epworth, 1963), a popular exposition addressed to a Methodist congregation. In 1965 he gave the Shaffer Lectures at Yale Divinity School, later published as *Jesus and the Gospel Tradition* (Philadelphia: Fortress, 1968).

The printed version of this lecture in honor of A. S. Peake (1865–1929), a noted Methodist biblical scholar in Britain, whose name is still known through the 1962 edition of a commentary he began, runs continuously, with no subheadings. Accordingly I have appended below a brief outline of Professor Barrett's own divisions, plus some supplemental references to items mentioned in his notes.

Lutheran Theological Seminary   JOHN REUMANN
Philadelphia, May, 1969

Contents

A. A. T. Ehrhardt's essay, discussed on pp. 32–36, has been reprinted in his collected works, *The Framework of the New Testament Stories* (Manchester Univ. Press, 1963; Cambridge, Mass.: Harvard Univ. Press, 1964), pp. 64–102.

The article cited on p. 21, note 24, by Joachim Jeremias, has been reprinted in his collected essays, *Abba: Studien zur neutestamentlichen Theologie und Zeitgeschichte* (Göttingen: Vandenhoeck & Ruprecht, 1966), pp. 238–55.

The essay by Käsemann, mentioned on pp. 25, 71, has also appeared in English under the title "Paul and Nascent Catholicism," in *Distinctive Protestant and Catholic Themes Reconsidered* ("Journal for Theology and the Church," 3; New York: Harper Torchbooks, 1967), pp. 14–27.

Preface

THERE is no student of the Bible who is not under some obligation to A. S. Peake, and it is a privilege to be able at least to acknowledge the debt through the Lecture established in his memory. I should like to express my thanks to the Trustees of the A. S. Peake Memorial Lecture, who have invited me to deliver the Lecture at the Methodist Conference of 1961.

It is much easier to revise and expand for publication a lecture one has already given than to write what is in effect a small book, part of which must be selected, six months or more after writing, for oral delivery. I cannot profess to know, as I write this Preface, how I shall select and dispose my material for the Lecture, but I am acutely aware of the fact that what I offer the reader in the following pages is a mixture containing some paragraphs written in a style intended for the ear, and others which are more suitable to the eye. I hope this will not be intolerably offensive.

There is more to apologize for. I have allowed myself the use of footnotes (incongruous though they are in a lecture), but even so the Lecture belies its title; it does not deal with one-twentieth of the recent study of the Lucan writings known to me, to say nothing of all that I do not know. As I look back, I can name several scholars whose work is of the highest importance, and ought to have been mentioned. I can only offer them my apologies, and say that, as it is, I have transgressed reasonable limits, and could not forgo the opportunity of making some comments of my own on a fascinating and important subject.

C. K. BARRETT

DURHAM
December, 1960.

Preface to the New Edition

The Select Bibliography appended to this new printing of *Luke the Historian in Recent Study* gives no more than a bare indication of the work done on the subject since I wrote the book eight years ago. It would be desirable now to rewrite the whole in the light of the latest discussions; circumstances forbid this, and I am content for the present to let the book reappear as it is, because though I might change it in detail I have no wish to modify the main lines on which the subject is treated. I hope to be able later to deal fully with Acts.

C. K. BARRETT

DURHAM
September, 1968.

Luke the Historian in Recent Study

'THE most beautiful book in the world.' The fact that the Third Gospel has survived this damning faint praise, pronounced by the learned but sentimental French rationalist Renan,[1] speaks well for its own vitality, and for that of its companion volume, the Acts of the Apostles. Whatever may have been true in Renan's time, we do not today continue to be interested in these books because we can find in them appealing stories of the gentle humanity of Jesus, and idyllic scenes from the tranquil existence of a youthful Church, free as yet from spot or wrinkle. To say this is not to pour cynical cold water on Luke's work; it is rather to pay him the compliment (which he would certainly have valued) of supposing that he was more concerned with truth than beauty —not least with the theological truth about Jesus and the historical truth about the Church.

That New Testament scholarship today is interested in Luke's work can be seen at once in the sudden rush of books and articles dealing with it which has marked the last few years.[2] Some of them will be mentioned in this Lecture, but before I speak of them explicitly I propose to illustrate the sort of question which the Lucan writings are now seen to evoke. In due course, when the questions have been briefly analysed, we shall look at some recent discussions of them; finally, I shall make a few comments of my own.

[1] 'C'est le plus beau livre qu'il y ait' (*Les Évangiles*; Paris, no date; p. 283). In this volume, however, and in others of his *Histoire des Origines du Christianisme*, Renan has remarks on Luke's work that are still worth pondering.

[2] E. Käsemann, in the Preface to his *Exegetische Versuche und Besinnungen* (Erster Band; Göttingen, 1960), speaks of 'dem plötzlich brennend gewordenen lukanischen Problem' (p. 8).

1. The first question that suggests itself to a reader of Luke-Acts[3] is one that I shall mention and then dismiss. In what text are we to read this work? In no other New Testament book is the problem so vexed. Nearly all the witnesses—manuscripts, versions, Fathers—fall into one or other of two great families, the Old Uncial text (represented notably by Codices Vaticanus and Sinaiticus) and the Western text (represented by Codex Bezae, the Latin versions, and the margin of the Harclean Syriac). We have here two textual types so clearly defined that it is hard to resist the view that we have to do with two different editions. Which is original, and which secondary? How did the secondary textual form arise? But the question must not be put in this form, which is so radically simplified that it must lead to a false answer. Granted that we have two distinct textual types, it need not be concluded that one is Luke's, the other that of a second-century editor. In all probability, each has something to contribute to our knowledge of Luke's text. There is much to be said for the view that the Old Uncial text stands on the whole nearer to what Luke wrote than does the Western text, but it can often be corrected by old readings which have been preserved in the Western text. Between them, the two texts give us an excellent idea of what Luke wrote,[4] but each verse, and each variant, must be treated on its merits, and without recourse to *a priori* judgements. This textual problem, however, if it were to be handled seriously, would require far more space than is available here, and I must be content to refer to the excellent critical accounts

---

[3] The term is inelegant, but I shall use it, both because it is convenient, and because it emphasizes that the Gospel and Acts are together one book.

[4] M. Dibelius (*Studies in the Acts of the Apostles*, edited by H. Greeven; English translation, London, 1956) suggests that the existence of the two texts reflects the early history of the book (pp. 98ff.).

of recent work on the subject by Dr A. F. J. Klijn.[5]

We may safely set aside the question of the text of Luke-Acts because, though the rival texts differ in many hundreds of places, the differences seldom amount to more than variations in word-order and the like, and there is rarely (though there is occasionally) serious question about what Luke meant to convey. Weightier and more difficult questions arise when we take up the Third Gospel and Acts, and begin to interrogate their form and content.

2. Both the form and the matter of his work place Luke among the historians; but we must not for that reason count him in the same company with Ranke and Acton, Meyer and Harnack. A historian of the modern scientific kind he certainly was not, but a historian of the Hellenistic age. His fellows are Polybius and Plutarch, Josephus and Tacitus. It is important to recognize this, though important also not to give it the wrong kind of emphasis. It does not mean that Luke is not to be taken seriously as a writer of history; the distinction between fact and fiction was understood long before he wrote. Moreover, we shall not forget that, if Luke is something less than a scientific historian, he is also something more; he is one of the biblical writers who confront us with a more than human testimony to Jesus Christ. Yet, true as this is, we shall understand Luke's testimony better if we recognize that as a man he shared, as it were by instinct, and brought to his task, the Hellenistic historian's conception of historiography. What was this conception? Later we must ask: How far did Luke share it?

We cannot give a simple answer to the question how the Hellenistic historian conceived his task, for no single conception of historiography prevailed in the Hellenistic age. Our space being limited, we cannot do better than

[5] *A Survey of the Researches into the Western Text of the Gospels and Acts* (Utrecht; no date (1949)); also *Novum Testamentum*, iii (1959), pp. 1-27, 161-73.

draw upon the little tract, 'On Writing History' by Lucian,
who was at work not long after the time of Luke. Lucian's
view of the nature and purpose of historical writing is
clear, and creditable to him: 'The one aim and goal of
history is, to be useful; and this can result only from its
truth' (9). 'The one task of the historian is to describe
things exactly as they happened' (39). 'This is the one
essential thing in history, to sacrifice to truth alone' (ibid.)
This is what Lucian has learnt from Thucydides; other
historians love to slip in here and there the Thucydidean
phrase, but to Lucian the name Thucydides means passion for truth. He recalls Thucydides's aim (1.22), to
write history not for passing entertainment but for per-
manent use (a κτῆμα ἐς ἀεί), neither ephemeral and
biased journalism nor *belles lettres*. Lucian adds, still
following Thucydides, that the historian must aim at accu-
racy and usefulness in order that, when similar circumstances recur, men may learn from the record of the past
how to act in present exigencies (42). This is Lucian at
his best, even though it may be a second-hand best, and
it is a lofty conception of the historian's duty that he sets
before his reader: scientific inquiry into the past with a
view to the greater wisdom of future generations. Lucian
himself, however, forbids us to suppose that all historians
of his day worked on these principles. His treatise opens
with an attack on his contemporaries, who try to mingle
in history the agreeable with the useful—generally, it
seems, with the emphasis upon the agreeable. 'Such are
the majority of historians who serve the present moment,
their own interest, and the profit they hope to get from
history' (13).

There are then two classes of historians: those who
write to please (and thus for their own profit), and those
who care for truth only. But the matter is not quite so
simple as that. For, first, Lucian would surely admit

that the reader *ought* to be pleased by the truth about the past which will instruct him in regard to the future; and, secondly, few historians, even the most honest, write without some conception of the nature of history, which is bound to affect their writing of it. Thus Lucian, and Thucydides himself, seem to imply a cyclic view of history; in the future there will appear similar conjunctions of circumstances to those which the historian relates.[6] Not only is it inevitable that history should be written on the basis of some presupposition about the nature of time; it is possible to write, and this means that it is all too easy to twist, history in the interest of a cause. On the whole, the Greeks were perhaps less prone to do this than the Romans; at least, the outstanding examples are Roman. In the Preface to his *History* Livy makes it clear that he has two causes to commend. First, the national cause: 'Whatever may come of my work, I shall at least have the joy of having played my part in perpetuating the memory of the first people in the world (*principis terrarum populi*); and if in the midst of so great a multitude of writers my fame remains in obscurity, I shall console myself with the glory and greatness of those who shall eclipse my repute.' Second, the cause of morals; 'This is the most wholesome and fruitful effect of the study of history; you have in front of you real examples of every kind of behaviour, real examples embodied in most conspicuous form; from these you can take, both for yourself and for the state, ideals at which to aim; you can learn also what to avoid because it is infamous either in its conception or in its issue.' It is precisely because his primary concern is for these two great causes that Livy does not distinguish too nicely between history and legend.

We may recall also Livy's greatest successor, Tacitus;

[6] See also the account of the πολιτειῶν ἀνακύκλωσις, the φύσεως οἰκονομία, καθ'ἣν μεταβάλλει καὶ μεθίσταται καὶ πάλιν εἰς αὐτὰ καταντᾷ τὰ κατὰ τὰς πολιτείας, in Polybius VI, v. 1-ix. 9 (the words quoted are from ix. 10).

an honest man if ever there was one, less of a moralist
and more of a rationalist, and not at all a jingo, but, as
is easily demonstrated, a historian who did not scruple
to rewrite an Emperor's speech for him,[7] and, still more
important, subconsciously allowed his political prejudice
to distort and misinterpret facts, which, with his conscious
mind, he was giving straightforwardly enough.[8]

This sketch of ancient historiography could be taken
much further, but space forbids; enough has already been
said to raise the question that concerns us. Beyond question, Luke was a historian of some kind; but of what
kind? Did he share Lucian's high ideals of objectivity, or
was he more concerned with his cause than with his facts?
This is not as simple a question as might appear, and it
is one to which we shall shortly hear more answers than
one.

3. Luke was a historical writer, and thus places himself in the midst of a group of historians. He was also a
religious writer, and thus places himself in a second
category. There were others in antiquity who told the
stories of religious personalities and religious communities, and Luke invites comparison with them. Three
groups of religious writers come under consideration, but
two of them may be quickly dismissed. First are the
gnostic writers, for whom religion and salvation consist
in the communication of divine knowledge. There is no
need to pursue this theme; no New Testament writer

[7] Tacitus gives the speech in *Annals*, xi. 24; the original is in an inscrip-
tion (Dessau 212).

[8] Tacitus is an outstanding example (worthy of careful notice by all
students of the New Testament) of the importance of a historian's selection
of his material. See F. B. Marsh, *The Reign of Tiberius* (London, 1931),
pp. 285-95; also M. P. Charlesworth, in *Cambridge Ancient History*, X (Cambridge, 1952), p. 627; also in the same volume pp. 871ff. ('Modern research
tends ultimately not so much to prove Tacitus false or malignant, but
rather to illustrate and stress aspects of the history of the Empire in which
Tacitus was not interested. Thus it comes about that the facts he reports
are usually accurate enough and rarely refuted by modern discoveries,
but his interpretation must often be challenged'; pp. 872f.).

shows fewer traces of gnosticism than Luke,[9] and he does not represent the Christians as a coterie of gnostics. Nor, secondly, does he represent Christianity as a mystery religion. His gospel is the story of a man's life, and in his pages the Church lives by the proclamation of the Word, not by the secret exercise of sacramental ritual. There is, however, a third class of religious literature and activity which may well be relevant to the Lucan writings, and that from both the literary and the religious viewpoints. The best examples are Philostratus's *Life of Apollonius of Tyana*, and Lucian's *False Prophet*,[10] the former a serious, the latter a caricatured picture of the religious expert, human yet more than human in his origin and person, who works miracles, proclaims a message, and gathers and teaches disciples. The figure of the divine man, accompanied by one or more disciples, was sufficiently familiar in the Hellenistic world, both in literature and in life. I shall take a few illustrations from the life of Apollonius. Anyone who will bear in mind the outstanding features of Luke-Acts will have no difficulty in grasping their significance.

Apollonius's birth was said to be supernatural. Before he was born, a divine being appeared to his mother (1.4). When she asked him what sort of child she was to bear, he answered, 'Myself.' 'Who are you?' she asked. 'Proteus, the god of Egypt,' was the reply. The child whose divine origin and nature were thus announced showed an unusual precocity in early youth. He had great beauty, strength of memory, and power of application; and was fortunate enough to speak, as it were instinctively, the best Attic Greek, without any trace of the local accent. No wonder that already all eyes were turned upon him.

His public ministry could be summed up by saying that he healed the sick, raised the dead, cast out demons,

[9] This does not mean that Luke was unaware of gnosticism; rather the contrary. See below, pp. 62f.
[10] See also Lucian's tract, *On the Death of Peregrinus*.

and preached the good news. There is for example the cure of a youth bitten by a mad dog at Tarsus (6.43); the raising of the dead girl at Rome, when he stopped the funeral procession in which the maiden's body was followed by her lamenting fiancé and her family, touched her and whispered over her, so that she woke up and spoke (4.45); the exorcism of the mocking demon at Athens, which proved its departure by knocking over a statue on the way (4.20); his early preaching at Antioch, when he conversed 'like a law-giver' ($\nu o \mu o \theta \acute{\epsilon} \tau \eta s$), and 'converted to himself the most uneducated people' (1.17).

In this way he made and instructed disciples (see his *Epistles*, 77, 81f., 84), though he did not encourage men to follow him without counting the cost (see especially 5.43). He was most unfavourably received in his own country, and by his own family. He writes to his brother, Hestiaeus: 'What marvel is it if, when other men think me to be equal with the gods, and some indeed think that I am a god, my own country ($\pi a \tau \rho \acute{\iota} s$) alone, for the sake of which I have striven to achieve fame, ignores me up to this moment? For, as I perceive, not even to you my brothers has it become clear that I am superior to the mass of men, both in speech and character' (*Epistle* 44). He is able, however, to escape when necessary from a hostile situation; for when he has appeared (in a Socratic role) before the Emperor Domitian he conveniently vanishes from the court, quoting Homer: 'You shall not kill me, for I am not mortal' (8.5; *Iliad*, 22.13).

In the end, after his death Apollonius proved himself alive by an appearance, in which he discoursed on immortality. It is not surprising that Philostratus never met with any tomb or cenotaph of the Wise Man (8.31).

It is a matter of fact that there is at least in form a resemblance between these stories and those which Luke tells in the first place about the Wise Physician of souls and bodies, and then about his followers (notably Peter and Paul). To say this is not to assert that there is no difference, or that Luke was incapable of perceiving a difference, between Jesus and Apollonius; the reverse of this is true. The observation may, however, teach us something about Luke, and about the way in which his writings should be studied and assessed. The Hellenistic romance[11] may make some claim to being the literary setting of the Lucan writings; and Hellenistic religion, which, at its worst, could be a shocking racket, mercilessly exploited by money-making charlatans, sharps, and pimps, but at its best was an honest attempt, by no means to be despised, to follow great souls on the path of life, may make a corresponding claim to furnish the social and religious background of Luke's story. To this point also we shall return.

4. So far I have considered one aspect only, the Hellenistic, of Luke's religious background. Luke himself was (it appears) a Gentile; but no New Testament writer is more clearly aware of the importance of the Old Testament, and of the Jews' religion. What is Luke's relationship with Judaism and the Old Testament?

One part of this question is so technical that, like textual criticism,[12] it must be mentioned and then set aside. How far, and in what sense, may Luke's language be described as Semitic? The Third Gospel and Acts are known to us in Greek; did they ever exist, in whole or in part, in Hebrew or Aramaic? The question may be considered in three special forms. (a) It is particularly acute in the Infancy Narratives of Luke 1, 2. No one can mistake the fact that after the thoroughly Greek periodic structure of the Preface (Luke 1[1-4]) we plunge

[11] See the excellent account of this body of literature by R. Helm: Der antike Roman (Göttingen; 2nd edition, 1956). The mainly biographical novel which traces the hero's fortunes through suffering to success is more relevant to the literary study of the New Testament than is sometimes recognized.

[12] See pp. 8f., above.

into a different world in which (one might almost say) Greek syntax is replaced by Semitic. Is this because Luke was translating a Semitic document, or because he was writing in a style (based on the LXX) suitable to his quasi-Old-Testament subject? Debate on this question continues.[13] (b) It is a common-place of small books on the Synoptic Gospels that Luke improves Mark's style, and the improvement is said to include the removal of Marcan Semitisms. This observation is not altogether false, but it is an inadequate account of the facts, for parts at least of the non-Marcan areas in Luke are as Semitic as Mark himself, and among the so-called Q passages in Luke there are some where the differences between Luke and Matthew have been more or less plausibly explained as translation variants. Was Luke himself less of a Hellenist than is sometimes thought, or were some of his sources in Hebrew or Aramaic? (c) The great Semitist C. C. Torrey[14] maintained that the whole of Acts 1-15 was a direct (and not always successful) translation from Aramaic. There are few who go all the way with Torrey. Some think that the Semitisms of Acts, as well as those of the gospel, are simply "Septuagintalisms';[15] others hold that the Semitisms are confined within a few passages, mainly in the speeches of the early chapters of Acts.[16] This last conclusion, if true, would

[13] Out of a great deal of literature we may note especially the contribution of P. Winter, including *Studia Theologica*, VII (1953-4), pp. 158-65; XII (1958), pp. 103-7; *Zeitschrift für die neutestamentliche Wissenschaft*, xlvi (1955), pp. 261ff.; xlvii (1956), pp. 217-42; *New Testament Studies*, i (1954), pp. 111-21. See also (for a different opinion) N. Turner in *New Testament Studies*, ii (1955), pp. 100-9.

[14] C. C. Torrey, *The Composition and Date of Acts* (Harvard Theological Studies I; Cambridge (U.S.A.), 1916).

[15] See especially H. F. D. Sparks in *Journal of Theological Studies* old series, xliv (1943), pp. 129-38 ('The Semitisms of St Luke's Gospel'); new series, i (1950), pp. 16-28 ('The Semitisms of the Acts').

[16] See the discussion by J. de Zwaan in *The Beginnings of Christianity*, II (London, 1922), pp. 30-65, especially p. 60; and the approval of de Zwaan's conclusions by C. H. Dodd in *The Apostolic Preaching and its Developments* (London, 1944), p. 20, n. 1.

be scarcely less important than Torrey's more wholesale opinion, for it would mean that the speeches attributed to Peter, though not necessarily authentic to him personally, come from the early Aramaic-speaking Church. Important as the matter is, it cannot be dealt with here, for even to set out the evidence without comment would call for study verse by verse and word by word. We must, however, bear the question in mind.

The study of the Semitic element in Luke's language calls for much detailed and difficult work, but even so it is scarcely so delicate a question as that of the Semitic element in Luke's thought. How can such a Semitic element, if present, be recognized? Where does Semitic thought differ from Greek?[17] Here I shall touch on only one aspect of the question, by way of illustration. I have already raised the question of Luke's place among the Hellenistic historians. It must be remembered, however, that though we are accustomed to speak of Herodotus as the 'Father of History', the Greeks were not the first, and certainly not the only, historians. Whether the statistical records of the oriental empires merit the title of history is open to question, but it is impossible to deny this description to the so-called Court History, in which some of the events of the reign of David, and Solomon's triumphant accession, are narrated. From the time of this work (probably the tenth century B.C.) not merely a historical tradition but a tradition of writing (as well as orally recounting) history persisted in Israel, and it was only in the later books of Maccabees that it was assimilated to the style (or styles) of Greek historiography— 1 Maccabees is still a Jewish book, written in the manner, though not at the high level, of the Old Testament.

It would be idle to pretend that the historical writing

[17] Here one may refer to T. Boman's *Hebrew Thought compared with Greek* (English translation, London, 1960), with which should be read R. Bultmann's review (of the German) in *Gnomon*, xxvii (1955), pp. 551-8.

B

of the Old Testament is marked by dispassionate objectivity. Its writers know which side they are on, and they
seldom make an attempt to see the point of view of Israel's
adversaries, or to be fair to them. Adversaries must be
destroyed, and the Lord hardens their hearts in order to
provide justification and occasion for their overthrow.
Nor do the historians scruple to include supernatural
events that may add glory to Israel's achievements or
facilitate the nation's enterprises. The sea turns back
and the sun stands still for the convenience of the Israelite
hosts. Behind, however, the naïveté of a pre-scientific
outlook on nature lies a quite serious view of the meaning
of history and of the way in which history should be
written. It is sometimes said that the Old Testament
writers used historical events in order to prove truths
about God and his relation with his people. This is not
so; if the Old Testament history books were designed for
this end, they were badly designed, for the story they tell
is consistent neither chronologically nor in theological
viewpoint, and can therefore *prove* nothing. The truth
is that the Old Testament writers did not need to use
history to prove certain doctrines about God. They wrote
history because they were convinced that they already
knew the truth about God and his relation with men, and
they wrote not as men concerned to establish a result
by their writing, but as men who had already reached
their conclusion and needed only to illustrate it, and
bear witness to it. How, and with what authority, the
Old Testament writers had reached their convictions
about God and his dealings with mankind, are questions
outside our scope; what we must observe is that they
wrote history as a confession of faith. This is true of all
the constituents of the Old Testament. 'Together with
the variety [in the Old Testament documents], there is
also a constant: a confession of faith in God's saving acts

on behalf of his people. This is present in individual passages, in the substance of the major sources, and in the framework of the completed compilation'.[18]

That Luke was familiar with the Old Testament, and with its manner of writing history, is beyond question. Quotations and style both make this certain. That he should have been affected by what he knew is at least a reasonable possibility. To say this is not to make the discussion of Greek historians and historical method irrelevant; it adds another component to the picture.[19] And what has been said of historiography might be said of other subjects too. Here I must simply reiterate the general question of which one illustration has now been given: What is Luke's relation to the Semitic element in the New Testament background?

5. We must narrow the framework of our examination of Luke, and study him in the light of his Christian background. Here again we are immediately confronted by a literary problem, to which it would be easy to devote a whole lecture, or series of lectures. What sources did Luke use in the composition of his two-volume book? In dealing with this question it is necessary to take the two volumes separately.

The gospel leads us into the field of synoptic criticism, and raises two special questions; first, that of the relation between Luke and Matthew, and second, that of the stages by which Luke came to its present form. The joint answer to these questions, which was popularized a generation ago by B. H. Streeter[20] and Dr Vincent

---

[18] G. W. Anderson, *A Critical Introduction to the Old Testament* (London, 1959), p. 237.

[19] It would be possible to add a further component by considering the historical material in the Dead Sea Scrolls, but I must be content here with a reference to the short note on pp. 24f. of *Biblical Problems and Biblical Preaching* ("Facet Books, Biblical Series," 6; Philadelphia, 1964).

[20] In *The Four Gospels* (London; first printed in 1924).

Taylor,[21] is that in the matter common to Matthew and Luke which has no parallel in Mark the two evangelists used a common documentary source, generally called Q; and that Luke's gospel came into being in two stages, in the first of which Q material was combined with matter peculiar to Luke (L), the result being a 'gospel' called by those who believe in its existence Proto-Luke, which was subsequently enriched by considerable insertions from Mark so as to produce the Third Gospel as we know it today. It is important to recognize that these two hypotheses hang together; take away the Q hypothesis, and the Proto-Luke hypothesis cannot stand. This means that the recent attacks upon the Q hypothesis[22] prove additionally to be attacks upon the theory that stages can be traced in the composition and literary history of Luke. If for example it is held that the relation between Matthew and Luke is better explained by supposing that each evangelist was independently engaged upon collecting gospel material and that they collected sometimes identical, and sometimes closely similar, traditional or literary units, this will have the consequence that there is no difference or discontinuity between Q (as Luke collected it) and L, except that what we call Q happened (independently and fortuitously) to be collected by Matthew also. From this it will follow that the occurrence in Luke of alternating blocks of Marcan and of Q + L material cannot bear the weight of argument that has been laid upon it. The gospel could appear in no other form; the First Gospel is substantially similar except that Matthew is accustomed to break up his sources into smaller pieces and rearrange them more

[21] *Behind the Third Gospel* (Oxford, 1926); *The First Draft of St Luke's Gospel* (London, 1927).

[22] For example, by B. C. Butler, *The Originality of St Matthew* (Cambridge, 1951); and by A. M. Farrer, 'On Dispensing with Q', in *Studies in the Gospels*, edited by D. E. Nineham (Oxford, 1955).

radically. I do not, however, wish here to establish a case so much as to indicate that recent discussions of Q have had the effect of reopening the question of Luke's sources and mode of composition, and to suggest that Luke's own words (Luke 1[1-4]) should be taken more seriously than it has of late been fashionable to take them: Luke knew that *many* had already attempted to write gospels, and he had himself collected material from an unspecified number of eye-witnesses and ministers of the Word.

When we turn from the gospel to Acts it is striking to note that though we have a second preface addressed to the same Theophilus there is no parallel to the words I have just referred to. In writing his gospel, Luke had many predecessors and sources of oral information; he could not claim such precedent and assistance for his second volume. An earlier generation (represented most notably by Harnack[23]) pursued the task of literary source analysis into the Acts, and with some show of *a priori* probability: an author who used written sources in his first volume would doubtless use them in his second also —if, we must add, they were available. Harnack was able to produce a neat and attractive theory which covered the early chapters of Acts and reached, more or less, the point at which Luke the companion of Paul was able to take over with his own knowledge and diary; but this theory is today generally abandoned[24] in favour

[23] *The Acts of the Apostles* (English translation, London, 1909), pp. 162-202.

[24] See, however, J. Jeremias, 'Untersuchungen zum Quellenproblem der Apostelgeschichte', *Zeitschrift für die neutestamentliche Wissenschaft*, xxxvi (1937), pp. 205-21. He sums up his conclusions on p. 221 as follows:
1. Die These, dass in Act 2-5 zwei parallel laufende Quellen verarbeitet seien, hält der Nachprüfung nicht stand.
2. Die einzige, mit einiger Wahrscheinlichkeit rekonstruierbare Quelle der Apg. umfasst die Stücke 6[1-8][4]; 9[1-30]; 11[19-30]; 12[25]-14[28]; 15[35ff].
3. Aus 2 ergibt sich, dass die erste Missionsreise erst *nach* dem Apostelkonzil stattfand.

of form-critical (or style-critical) analysis. The new method has greater probability on its side. In what circumstances, and for what purposes, can we imagine the churches of Jerusalem and Antioch keeping minute-books in the first decade of their existence, or compiling archives?[25] Who could distinguish between a source written up in his own style by Luke, and a narrative written by him in the first instance, on the basis of collected information? Two reasonably firm points are these. (a) In the later chapters, the author occasionally uses the first person plural. It is wildly improbable that this is merely a device of fiction, which the author used when he remembered to do so, but more often forgot. This means, not necessarily that the author was an eye-witness but that he had some sort of access to some sort of eye-witness material for this part of his narrative. (b) The speeches and sermons of the early chapters seem to be separable from their contexts; that is, the narrative matter and the spoken matter have different origins, and were presumably put together by the compiler. This observation leads us back, by stylistic considerations, to Luke's intention and method as a historian; for in speaking of his relation with his Christian background our interest is not primarily literary.

Luke himself stands at a point (a point very difficult to settle in chronological terms) in the development of early Christianity; what is his total attitude, conscious and unconscious, to the time before his own? At this stage, I have two preliminary observations to make. (a) Luke's picture of Jesus is superficially clearer and simpler than Mark's. It is not for nothing that the Third Gospel has always been the stronghold of the liberal humanitarian interpretation of Jesus. He appears, or with only a very little manipulation can be made to appear, as man

[25] See W. L. Knox, *The Acts of the Apostles* (Cambridge, 1948), pp. 21, 27.

among men, marked by a ready compassion and gentle simplicity of character, a person who, though he must in the end lay down his life in a martyr's death, is free of theological complication. This gospel is not over-shadowed, as Mark's is, by the theme of secrecy, the inexorable necessity of suffering, and the grim solitude in which Jesus moves forward to death. He is the 'good, the kind Physician', loved in his life and lamented in his death. J. M. Creed's well-known dictum, 'There is in-deed [in Luke] no *theologia crucis* beyond the affirmation that the Christ must suffer, since so the prophetic scrip-tures had foretold',[26] is not the whole truth, but it is not lightly to be set aside. The fact is that Luke stands far enough from the historical Jesus to have digested the raw, perplexing traditions which stand in Mark in all their crudity and offensiveness, and to have made of them something less scandalous, and more easily assimi-lable. (*b*) By contrast, Acts is full of obscurity and diffi-culty, as anyone will readily detect who attempts to reconstruct, for example, a clear picture of how baptism was practised, and what was believed about it, in the earliest Church, or of the way in which the Church ex-panded so as eventually to include the Gentiles. How were water-baptism and Spirit-baptism related to each other? Did the rite of immersion require the laying on of hands for its completion? Did the gift of the Spirit pre-cede, accompany, or follow baptism? How was baptism related to the forgiveness of sins, and to eschatology? Again, was it clear from the first that the apostles were to preach in Jerusalem, Judaea, Samaria, and up to the ends of the earth (Acts 1[8])? If so, why were they so hesitant in obeying their orders? How is it that in Acts 9 disciples appear without explanation in Lydda, Joppa, and distant Damascus? If it was settled in Acts 10, 11

[26] *The Gospel according to St Luke* (London, 1930), p. lxxii.

that lack of circumcision was no barrier either to baptism or to table-fellowship, why was it necessary to
discuss the matter again in Acts 15? It is anomalies
such as these that lead to, and in large measure justify,
the charge that Acts is remote and vague in its treatment
of the earliest history of the Church, its beliefs, and its
institutions. The reason for this remoteness and for these
conflicting statements is not hard to find. Luke was
describing one age of the Church, and that a unique one,
with the presuppositions of another. For him, baptism
was the established mode of initiation into a religious
community; a generation earlier it had been John's
eschatological sacrament transposed in the light of the
death and resurrection of Jesus. For Luke and the
Church of his day, the position of Gentiles was assured
and unquestioned; it was hard for him to enter into the
theological revolution, and the personal conflicts, which,
in an earlier generation, had made it possible for Gentiles to hear the Gospel at all. The interplay, however,
in Luke's work of the contemporary Christian scene and
the tradition which he drew from the past, constitutes
one of the subjects[27] on which we shall hear more later.
For the present we may use it simply as a transition to
the last of the subjects we shall touch on in this preliminary sketch.

6. Luke offers us two pictures of the Church, one consciously and intentionally, the other accidentally and un-
consciously. He sets out to depict the Church of the first
few decades, in its relationship with Jesus himself. This
picture we read straight out of his books. It may or may
not be an accurate picture—that remains open to discussion. At any rate, it is there for all to see. But un-
consciously Luke depicts for us also the Church of his

[27] A special aspect of this question is Luke's treatment of Paul. The
trustworthiness of Luke's account of Paul is not discussed in this lecture,
but see p. 63.

own time. He does this, as we have seen, by reading back into the past its assumptions and presuppositions, and also by his selection and arrangement of material. The result is that his work sometimes gives us the impression of a screen upon which two pictures are being projected at the same time—a picture of the Church of the first period, and, superimposed upon it, a picture of his own times.

It is not to Luke's discredit that he thus betrayed his own circumstances in his historical writing; no man can detach himself from his own environment, and Luke probably did not attempt to do so. The question we must consider, and for the present I shall be content to state it very briefly, is, What sort of ecclesiastical background becomes visible through the Lucan writings? The answer has been given, Primitive catholicism;[28] but this answer only repeats the question unless one has a clear understanding of what 'primitive catholicism' was. The answer surely is a correct one if 'primitive catholicism' is defined in the very careful terms used by Dr Käsemann himself, as 'nothing other than the Church's defensive movement against the threat of gnosticizing'.[29] But even this careful definition leaves much undefined. By what means did the Church try to defend itself against the threat of gnosticism? Several different methods were adopted, and they do not all appear in Luke-Acts. It is an important part, therefore, of our task to observe which of these were and which were not used by Luke, and to inquire why he used some and neglected others. This, however, is a task that lies ahead of us, and we must not pursue it now. For the present we must be content to ask the question in more open terms. We have looked at Luke's connection *backward* with the primitive Church of

28 *Frühkatholizismus*. See E. Käsemann, *ZThK*, liv (1957), p. 20, reprinted in *Exegetische Versuche und Besinnungen*, II (Göttingen, 1964), p. 29; Eng. trans. by W. J. Montague, *New Testament Questions of Today* (Philadelphia, 1969), p. 21.

29 Ibid.

the first decades; what may be said of his connection *forward*
with the developed Christianity of the second century?

We have now considered six questions which are raised
when we look at the two great works that Luke has left
us. They are far more important than such naïve in-
quiries as, Who was their author? We may continue to
call him Luke. The vital questions are: What did Luke
intend to do? And what did he in fact achieve? These
questions may easily be analysed into the particular
topics I have suggested. What made Luke embark upon
religious history? What were his ideas of religion and of
history? What does he reveal to us intentionally, and
what does he reveal to us unintentionally, of the life of
the Church in and before his own day? In raising these
questions I have done my best to proceed on the basis
of the New Testament data—to raise, that is, the questions which the documents themselves raise. It would,
however, be both foolish and ungrateful to pretend that
I have not been prompted by many recent writers, and
I now proceed, in the second part of this lecture, to show
what contributions six of these writers have made to the
elucidation of the problems they have helped to expose.

1. No one has done more to turn the study of the Lucan
writings into new and fruitful paths than Martin Dibelius,
whose lamentably early death took place in 1947. His
work on Acts has been conveniently collected into a
volume of essays, and translated into English.[30] It forms
a suitable starting-point for the sketch of modern work
on Luke on which we are now embarking.

Dibelius is best known in England as one of the founders
of the form-critical method in the study of the gospels.[31]
When, however, he turned to Acts he spoke not of form

[30] See n. 4 on p. 8.
[31] See especially *From Tradition to Gospel* (English translation; London,
1934).

criticism (*Formgeschichte*) but of style criticism (*Stilkritik*). For, notwithstanding the real and indisputable unity between the Third Gospel and Acts, Luke was compelled to proceed in the latter volume on different lines from those he followed in the former. It was the material itself that demanded this change. In the gospel he might be (like Matthew and Mark) an arranger of traditional material which had already come to exist in a number of fairly well defined forms; but for the history of the primitive Church there was no such formulated tradition. In the second volume, Luke is no longer merely a compiler of traditions, but an author. To say this is not to imply that he made up his material out of his head, and wrote it all out flowingly in a book marked by linguistic unity. On the contrary, it is possible to detect varieties of style in Acts, and it is with this process of detection that criticism must be concerned, rather than with the older kind of attempt to break the narrative down into a few sources.

'The question as to what is tradition and what is the author's own composition has to be repeated with reference to each section' (Dibelius, *Studies*, p. 11), and in his earliest article Dibelius carries this out for the isolable short narratives of Acts: the raising of Tabitha, the story of Cornelius, the lame man at the gate of the Temple, the story of Pentecost, the conversion of the Eunuch, Ananias and Sapphira, Elymas, Simon the sorcerer, the revival of Eutychus, the sons of Scaeva, the death of Herod, the escape at Malta, the healing at Lystra, Peter's release, and the escape of Paul and Silas at Philippi. The analysis of these units leads to various results. It is for example useless to seek traditional material in the story of Pentecost; 'the part contributed by the author is considerable' (op. cit., p. 15). There are stories of secular, that is, of non-Christian origin, such as that of the sons of Scaeva, and the record of Herod's unhappy end. There

are legends (whose characteristic is that they show interest in people, especially in outstanding characters),
such as those of Peter, Cornelius, and the Eunuch; sometimes there is a subordinate, 'devotional' (*fromm*) interest
in subsidiary characters, such as Ananias and Sapphira.
There are stories of the type which, in the gospels, Dibelius
calls Tales (*Novellen*). To this class belongs the story of
the lame man in the Temple, where there is no attempt
either to edify, or to characterize the persons in the story.
No more than in the gospels can formal or stylistic classi-
fication in itself settle the question of historicity, but it
helps the student to distinguish between the author's own
work and the material upon which he was working, and
this is the first step both to the assessment of historical
truth, and to interpretation.

In the stylistic analysis of Acts the speeches play an
important part. To understand them, we must remem-
ber that Luke belongs within the framework not of
modern but of ancient historiography, and the old historians used speeches not as verbatim reports of things
actually said but to convey to the reader insights into
various aspects of their subject. These may be

1. An insight into the total situation. . . .
2. An insight into the meaning of the historical moment concerned, but one which goes beyond the facts of history. Even
though the insight may not have been revealed to the historical character at the moment when he is making the
speech, the writer nevertheless lets him supply it.
3. An insight into the character of the speaker.
4. An insight into general ideas which are introduced to explain the situation . . .(op. cit., pp. 139f.).

How do the speeches of Acts fit into this framework of
contemporary method? Paul's speech at Athens forms a
good starting-point, precisely because, to judge from the
epistles, Athens was not an important Pauline centre. It

must be Luke himself who has placed the sermon there, and the sermon is probably Luke's own work—a conclusion borne out by the fact that it smacks more of Hellenistic philosophy than of Paul's theology. It was intended to represent Paul as the apostle of the Gentiles. Similarly, the speech made by Paul in Miletus to the Ephesian elders paints the picture of Paul that Luke wishes us to see. Other speeches may be analysed in the same way, but in some the interest lies rather in what is said than in the historical or biographical setting. Such are the speeches of Peter in the early chapters, where the motive is, 'This is how the Gospel is preached and ought to be preached!' (op. cit., p. 165). Luke intends to preach the Gospel to his readers, and thus it is the Gospel as he understands it that he puts into the mouth of the apostles. Dibelius's conclusions are best given in his own words (op. cit., p. 183):

By comparing the speeches in Acts with those of the historians we observe an important ambiguity. Luke indeed uses the historical technique and does set himself certain historical aims; this becomes clear enough when we give up trying to measure him by our ideas of historiography and historians. In the last analysis, however, he is not a historian but a preacher; we must not allow our attempts to prove the authenticity of the speeches to cloud our perception of their kerygmatic nature.

This recalls the stress laid by Dibelius on preaching as the *Sitz im Leben* in which the gospel material was preserved. 'Missionary purpose was the cause and preaching was the means of spreading abroad that which the disciples of Jesus possessed as recollections'.[32] He says with special reference to Luke:[33]

Luke's Prologue indicates the limits of the significance which tradition has for preaching. The author wishes to give to the

[32] *From Tradition to Gospel*, p. 13.   [33] Ibid., p. 15.

Theophilus who is mentioned in the dedication a more certain account concerning the things which he had learned from the didactic and missionary preaching. Luke's gospel contains, not the content of the preaching, but a guarantee for that content.

Acts thus appears as an artistic work, fundamentally a preaching of the Gospel by Luke in and for his own time, but enriched with biographical interest that shades off into legend, the Third Gospel as a more traditional document, presenting the historical traditions on which the Church's preaching rested.

2. Dr Bertil Gärtner's discussion of *The Areopagus Speech and Natural Revelation*[34] would be prejudiced from the start if he were obliged to proceed from Dibelius's conclusions regarding the origin of the speech. He calls them in question in an introductory chapter headed 'The Greek and the Jewish Type of Historical Writing', which leads to an assessment of 'St Luke as a Historian'. Like Dibelius, Dr Gärtner discusses at some length the Greek historians, with their presuppositions and methods; unlike Dibelius, he adds an account of historical writing in the Old Testament, and in the Maccabean Books and Josephus. Luke, says Dr Gärtner, follows the Jewish tradition in that 'he looks at the course of events from a religious standpoint' (op. cit., p. 26). This is evident enough; it is also reasonably certain, as Dr Gärtner adds, that Luke was prompted to write by the situation of the Church in his own time, though by no means so certain (it seems to me) that his motive was to defend the Church against charges of sedition. Turning to the speeches, Dr Gärtner recalls Dibelius's analysis of them into two categories, one containing speeches analogous to those of the Greek historians, and one containing missionary speeches. Provisionally accepting the analysis, Dr Gärtner

[34] Uppsala, 1955.

questions Dibelius's conclusions with regard to each class.

The proper setting for Acts and its speeches is not the Greek tradition of historiography but the Jewish. Dibelius's 'first group of speeches [those alleged to be intelligible on the basis of ancient historical writing] show almost nothing of the contemporary stylistic ideal, and are not nearly so elaborated' (op. cit., p. 28). The speeches have an apologetic and didactic motive, connected with the purpose for which the book was written. Whereas the Jew Josephus adhered to the Greek style of writing, the Gentile Luke stands closer to 1 and 2 Maccabees. The speeches of Dibelius's second group (the missionary sermons) reflect (as do the speeches in non-Christian historians) contemporary oratory; what this means is that we find in them a type of sermon which had been evolved during the expansion of the Christian mission in the time of the apostles. Seven articles can be distinguished in the preaching addressed to Jews:

1. The ministry of Jesus, His suffering, death, and resurrection.
2. The fulfilment in these events of the prophecies.
3. Jesus is now Lord and Messiah, exalted to the right hand of God; he gives the Holy Spirit.
4. The apostolic message extends to the Gentiles also.
5. The expectation of the Advent and the Judgement.
6. The exhortation to conversion.
7. The bearing of witness.

These seven articles are all represented in the Pauline epistles, and from this observation Dr Gärtner (differing from Dibelius) concludes 'that the sermon type found in the Acts exemplifies the apostolic message as promulgated by Peter and Paul' (op. cit., p. 33). 'There is no doubt that [Luke] gave them their outer form, but this does not prevent us from thinking that he had reliable sources, and that he really gives specimens of the apostolic

message' (ibid.). Small personal distinctions between the
speeches attributed to Peter and Paul respectively may
be observed. Stephen's speech is also a missionary sermon, exemplifying a Christian Hellenistic propaganda;
so is the speech in Athens, which is directed to a Gentile
and intellectual public. Thus, what Acts gives us is
'three types of missionary sermon: those represented by
the message of Peter and Paul to the Jews, the "propaganda speech" by Stephen, and Paul's preaching to the
Gentiles. As a fourth type, we might take Paul's farewell speech in Ephesus, which shows elements of "community preaching" and of "testament" ' (op. cit., p. 35).
Less certainly, but not unreasonably, we may also place
some confidence in the historical settings Luke supplies
for the speeches.

It is on the basis of these general observations and con-
servative conclusions that Dr Gärtner goes on to examine
Paul's Areopagus speech in detail.

3. Another writer fundamentally critical of Dibelius is
Dr Arnold Ehrhardt, who deals with the construction and
purpose of Acts.[35] Dr Ehrhardt holds a high view of Luke
as a historical writer; he refers to Eduard Meyer's appraisal of him as the one great historian between Polybius,
last of the genuinely Greek historians, and Eusebius, the
first great Christian historian. He was no mere collector
of trifles, but told the history of the early years of Christianity. Nevertheless, he was not a historian in the Greek
tradition; he practised the characteristically Jewish
method of historical biography, and it is this method
that must be traced and assessed in his work. The opening chapters of Acts, for example, continue the story,
begun in the gospel, of the growth and development of
Peter. He learns to stand alone—or rather, to rely on

---

[35] 'The Construction and Purpose of the Acts of the Apostles', in *Studia
Theologica*, XII (1958), pp. 45-79.

God only; this, according to Dr Ehrhardt, is why in the earliest chapters Peter is always accompanied by John (though John contributes nothing to the stories), whereas later John disappears. He makes the suggestion that the true significance of the story of the centurion Cornelius is 'the conversion of—St Peter' (op. cit., p. 50, n. 1). The portrait of Peter is achieved, like all good portraits, by the art of omission. Why then (Dr Ehrhardt asks) did Luke, who omitted so many conflicts, record the contention between Paul and Barnabas? Because he intended to make and mark the break between the first part of his book, which is centred in the Jerusalem Church, and the second, which is centred in Paul. At the same time Luke maintains the essential unity of his book by underlining the links between the leader of Gentile Christianity and the Church at Jerusalem. This is done in three ways: (1) 'Saul . . . is brought as near to the martyrdom of St Stephen as historical truth will permit' (op. cit., p. 52). (2) Paul's work is introduced by Philip's mission in Samaria and his baptism of the Eunuch, and also (3) by the 'miraculous acceptance of the uncircumcised Cornelius . . . by the Holy Spirit in the presence of St Peter' (op. cit., p. 53). Luke thus applies his biographical art in describing the growth of Peter's personality, and in emphasizing the connection between Paul and the Jerusalem Church. In this description there is both an 'intrinsic verity' and a 'marked consistency of purpose' (op. cit., p. 54).

Dr Ehrhardt turns to Luke's technique. Acts is not simply an apology, claiming that Christianity is a harmless religion which may properly be tolerated by the Empire. Luke wrote under the pressure of the Holy Spirit, and of the impending *parousia* of Jesus Christ. His characters are not purely finite beings. 'St Peter, St Stephen, St Philip, St Paul, St Barnabas, or James are

C

not so much fascinating characters as characters in the Divine tragedy; and this tragedy is the Gospel of the Spirit of God' (op. cit., p. 57).

Luke's technique is illustrated by discussion of two subjects to which we have already given some attention: the sources of Acts, and the speeches. Dr Ehrhardt begins his discussion of the sources from the 'we-passages' in the latter part of the book. It is difficult to dispute the view that the inclusion of these sections cast in the first person plural is intended to suggest that the author of Acts 16-28 (and probably of the book as a whole) was a travelling companion of Paul's, probably 'Luke the beloved physician'. This leaves the reader with a plain choice; he may either accept this suggestion, made by the book itself, as true, or reject it, preferring the view that the book is a forgery (Dr Ehrhardt insists upon this word). Two main arguments (says Dr Ehrhardt) are alleged in favour of the latter alternative. (1) 'The events reported in Acts are difficult to square with the hints to be found in St Paul's Epistles' (op. cit., p. 62). If it is allowed that Luke pruned the evidence in the interests of his theological purpose this objection loses weight. (2) It is argued that Acts 5[36] shows that the author had read Josephus's *Antiquities*, and therefore wrote at so late a date that he could not have been one of the Pauline circle. A poor argument; the author may have used Josephus's source.[36] These arguments failing, the former alternative may be preferred.

---

[36] I must admit that I am unable to follow another reason given by Dr Ehrhardt for rejecting the conclusion that Acts 5[36] proves that Acts was written as late as A.D. 100, and therefore not by Luke. The reason is that by A.D. 100 the Pauline epistles were already widely read. They contributed to "the extraordinary medley of New Testament phrases and heathen religious and astrological language which forms the Greek of Ignatius" [W. L. Knox] of Antioch. At the same time the Antiochene origin of Acts is more than a mere conjecture; and thus its author must have finished his work some time before Ignatius, whose martyrdom took place at the latest in A.D. 117' (op. cit., p. 65).

Dr Ehrhardt thinks that Luke did not freely invent speeches (though he may sometimes have turned historical reports into direct speech); he misses too many opportunities of inserting speeches which he surely would have used had he been writing the speeches himself, and when he manifestly does write a speech (Gamaliel's) it is notably unsuccessful and does not bear comparison with the other speeches, which presumably therefore Luke did not write.

Dr Ehrhardt considers last the purpose of Acts. In a word, the book was intended to serve as 'the Gospel of the Holy Spirit' (op. cit., p. 67). He expounds this purpose in four points. (1) 'The whole doctrine of the Catholic Church concerning the Holy Spirit rests upon the prominent place accorded to His coming on the day of Pentecost, in the second chapter of Acts' (op. cit., p. 68). This is a sweeping statement, and Dr Ehrhardt seems not unnaturally anxious to show that he is aware that the Spirit is mentioned also in other New Testament writings, such as those of Paul and John. (2) 'It was the Primitive Church at Jerusalem which found itself, according to Acts, as the trustee of the Holy Spirit' (ibid.). This observation begins, like the last, from the events at Pentecost; another instance is found in Stephen, 'a man full of the Holy Spirit', and a third in the relation between the Church and the Temple: it is when the time of the Temple is past that the Holy Spirit (cf. Luke 1, 2) can be poured out on all flesh. For this reason the church at Jerusalem exercises control over foreign missions, though the Cornelius episode comes as a salutary reminder that 'the Holy Spirit is God, and He is free' (op. cit., p. 71). (3) Dr Ehrhardt reiterates the importance for Acts of the connection between Paul and Jerusalem. Paul was one of the greatest assets of the Jerusalem Church, for (against the different emphases of other less 'Catholic' parts of

Christendom) he always insisted upon the importance of the Spirit (Acts 18, 19). (4) 'The Holy Spirit completed the construction of the Catholic Church, originating from Jerusalem, by sending the Apostle to Rome from the birth-place of the Church' (op. cit., p. 75). This makes sense of the ending of Acts,[37] as well as of the significant statement (Acts 16[6-10]) that the Holy Spirit sent Paul into Macedonia—into Europe. It is as the ambassador of the Church of the Holy Spirit, and in the power of the Spirit, that Paul reaches Rome.

A final judgement of Luke as a historian needs to be carefully balanced. Even an eye-witness may not be strictly accurate twenty years after the event; but Luke used written sources, which shows that he believed he was recording (even in the earlier chapters) what really happened, though he selected his material in accordance with his purpose.

4. A large-scale attempt to do justice to the complexity of Luke's work, in both volumes of his history, was made by Dr Robert Morgenthaler.[38] His work falls into two parts, in which he considers first the form, then the content, of the Lucan writings. All proceeds from the observation that, as is very generally allowed, Luke's writing is artistic, his work a work of art (*Kunst*). The questions that must be answered are: How does Luke the artist use his material? And how does his artistic writing affect the historical and theological value of his books?

The first part of the answer is that Luke builds his work on a principle of doubling, or of pairs—Dr Morgenthaler's word, not easy to translate simply, is *Zweigliedrigkeit*. He quotes a saying of Bussmann's: 'Luke has the

[37] Why does Luke end his work with Paul's residence in Rome, and make no reference to the further activity, or martyrdom, of Paul and Peter? If we do not accept the view that Luke stops writing because he has brought his book up to date, some explanation of the end of Acts must be given.

[38] *Die lukanische Geschichtsschreibung als Zeugnis*, two volumes (Zürich, 1949).

greatest number of doublets of all the Synoptics, so far removed is he from any dread of doublets' (op. cit., i, p. 13),[39] and proceeds to work out this observation in the greatest detail, with reference to words, sentences, paragraphs, and overall composition. The evidence, drawn from both gospel and Acts, is impressive in quantity, perhaps rather less impressive and convincing in quality. For example, in the discussion of words, not all the alleged tautologies are really tautologous; in Luke 9^1 δύναμις and ἐξουσία may be synonymous, or nearly so, but in 22^{53} ὥρα and ἐξουσία are not; in Acts 5^{15} κλινάρια and κράβατοι are scarcely to be distinguished, but in 17^{18} the word ἀνάστασις makes a clear addition to the name Ἰησοῦς. Nevertheless, when a certain amount of the material has been discounted, a good deal remains. For our purpose, the most important section of Dr Morgenthaler's discussion is his treatment of the plan of the whole two-volume work. It may (he says) be broadly analysed as follows:

Scenes in Jerusalem I	Luke 1^5-4^{13}
Travel Narrative I	4^{14}-19^{44}
Scenes in Jerusalem II	19^{45}-24^{53}
Scenes in Jerusalem III	Acts 1^4-7^{60}
Travel Narrative II	8^1-21^{17}
Scenes in Jerusalem IV	21^{18}-26^{32}
Travel Narrative III	27^1-28^{31}

On the basis of this general account, Dr Morgenthaler goes on to show in detail that the first two sets of Jerusalem scenes (which are separated by a section clearly marked off by geographical location as well as by the kind of material it contains) correspond closely to each other. He sums up: 'In the one, the Christ is born in

[39] See W. Bussmann, *Synoptische Studien*, I (Halle, 1925), p. 57. Bussmann conducts a long argument (pp. 6-66) against Luke's alleged *Duplettenfurcht*.

poverty; in the other He suffers and dies. In the one, He is in His humanity tempted by Satan; in the other, it is the same. In the one, the Son of God through birth becomes man, in the other through the resurrection He is again exalted. As in the one John is rejected, so in the other is Jesus; and so forth' (op. cit., i, p. 168). The intervening travel narrative falls into two parts. In 4^{14}-9^{51} Jesus simply wanders through Palestine with no further intention than that of preaching the Gospel everywhere; from 9^{51} onwards his face is set towards Jerusalem. These two divisions of the travel narrative can be shown to contain numerous correspondences. Each begins with a rejection. At the beginning of the former stands the call of the tax-collector Levi, at the end of the latter that of the tax-collector Zacchaeus. At the end of the former Jesus proclaims His approaching passion; He does so again at the end of the latter. Each contains two deeds wrought on the Sabbath. Thus the Gospel can be more completely analysed thus:

Scene I:	Jerusalem narratives	1^{5}-4^{13}
Scene II:	On the road (in Galilee)	4^{14}-9^{50}
Scene III:	On the road (in Samaria) to Jerusalem	9^{51}-19^{44}
Scene IV:	Jerusalem narratives	19^{45}-24^{53}

Dr Morgenthaler next works out parallels between these Jerusalem and travel sections in the gospel with those in Acts. The same pattern of 'two-foldness', and with it the same themes, of the fulfilment of Judaism, and the rejection by Judaism of its own fulfilment, together with the acceptance of the Gentiles, runs throughout the whole work. 'That is the meaning of the overall composition of the Lucan writings: the Jewish question, or the Gentile question—it all depends on the direction in which one looks' (op. cit., i, p. 190).

Why does Luke choose to build up his artistic work on this principle of two-foldness (varied occasionally by three-foldness)? The answer is given in Dr Morgenthaler's second volume, in the observation that Luke intends by means of his work to bear witness, and it is laid down in Scripture (Deut. 19[15]; cf. Matt. 18[16ff.]; 2 Cor. 13[1]; 1 Tim. 5[19]; Heb. 10[28]; 1 John 5[6ff.]) that testimony is to be received *at the mouth of two or three witnesses*.[40] Hence Luke's tautologies, doublets, and repetitions. And, more important, hence also a vindication of Luke's character as a historian. The trustworthiness of the Lucan histories has been attacked, according to Dr Morgenthaler, on two main lines, which he neatly, and not inaccurately, summarizes thus (op. cit., ii, p. 25):

1. Luke's historical writing is a work of art, but is not truly historical; for art has to do with aesthetics, and has nothing at all to do with crude historicity.
2. Luke's historical writing is testimony, but is by no means truly historical; for testimony has to do with theology, and has nothing at all to do with crude historicity.

But Luke's art is the art of two-foldness (and three-foldness), and this shows that the only kind of testimony Luke means to offer is that which would satisfy a law-court, which demands twofold and threefold testimony. Luke is narrating a redemptive history (*Heilsgeschichte*), and this means that he is speaking of a historical (*geschichtlich*) redemption. This observation is more important than comparisons between Luke and other ancient historians.[41] Luke was well equipped to write history, and the form his history took arose not out of his imagination

[40] On this theme see H. van Vliet, *No Single Testimony* (Utrecht, 1958), especially n. 19.

[41] Cf. below, p. 61. It would not, however, follow from this observation that the examination of historical models is valueless in the study of Acts.

but out of the historical event itself. Dr Morgenthaler applies to Luke's work as a whole words written by Schlatter with reference to Luke 1 (op. cit., ii, p. 110): 'This narrative has often been called a poem. Were that the whole truth, he who wrote it would be among the greatest who ever received the poetic gift. But there is divine poetry as well as human; and more poetic than all poetry is the history which the Spirit of God brings about.'

5. Another book that deals with the Lucan writings as a whole is Dr Hans Conzelmann's *Die Mitte der Zeit*,[42] a book which must be regarded as the outstanding modern assessment of Lucan theology. It falls into five parts, of which the first is the hardest to summarize, for in it Dr Conzelmann surveys rapidly the gospel material as a whole, treating each pericope or larger unit in turn and assessing its significance for his inquiry into Luke's theological presuppositions, methods, and results. Here we must be content with a few illustrative examples. Dr Conzelmann deals first with John the Baptist. Except in the nativity stories Luke recognizes no typological correspondence between John and Jesus. John does not appear as a forerunner, as Elijah, or as a sign of the advent. He is a prophet, a preacher of repentance, and thus a representative of the former age. In him and Jesus two periods in the one history of redemption (*Heilsgeschichte*) come together at their common boundary; but the two men stand on opposite sides of the frontier. It is John's work and not his person that prepares the way for Jesus. 'In this way John acquires a clearly defined function in the *middle* of the *Heilsgeschichte*. If it is his ministry, not his existence, that is the preparation for Jesus, then he is subordinated to the work of Jesus in the same way

[42] Tübingen, 1954; revised edition, 1960. An English translation has been published during the writing of this lecture: *The Theology of St Luke* (London, 1960).

as the whole epoch of the Law' (op. cit., p. 15). For example, his death is the death of a prophet, not an eschatological event (cf. Luke 9[9] with Mark 9[12f.]).

Dr Conzelmann's treatment of the ministry of Jesus himself may be represented by his discussion of a characteristic passage, Luke 4[16-30].

The theme Promise-Fulfilment is set forth by means of two biblical quotations. The first, in vv. 18f., expressly announces fulfilment in the 'Present'. Schlatter (221)[43] describes its content thus: 'What Jesus said to the men of Nazareth was the Gospel, without veil. He brings them the time of salvation (*Heilszeit*).' One recalls 2 Cor. 6[2]: ἰδοὺ νῦν καιρὸς εὐπρόσδεκτός. But when Luke makes Jesus say: σήμερον πεπλήρωται ἡ γραφὴ αὕτη, the distinction becomes clear: Paul describes his *own* as the eschatological time, but Luke sees salvation already in the past. The time of salvation has become historic, a period of time which certainly determines the present, but as an epoch is past and closed. That Luke is clear about this matter is shown by the analogous paragraph 22[35f.], which sets over against each other the time of Jesus and the present. This signifies neither more nor less than the conception that the time of the End (*Endzeit*) did not break in with Jesus. Rather, the future time of salvation was portrayed in advance in the middle of the *Heilsgeschichte* in the life of Jesus. This is a portrayal which even now establishes our hope; more, it is an event which gives us forgiveness and

Lucan eschatology. If we wish to understand Luke's own
eschatological thinking (as distinct from that of Jesus or
of the earliest Church), what we must look for is tension
or discrepancy between his sources and his editing of
them. An example may be found in the quotation from
Joel in Acts 2[17ff.]. Naturally, Luke as well as his source
takes the quotation to mean that the gift of the Spirit is
a sign of the last time, but whereas for the source, the
'last days' are truly the End, for Luke himself they stretch
out into a continuous tract of history, so that 'the out-
pouring of the Spirit is no longer in itself the *Eschaton*,
but the opening of a lengthy epoch, the time of the Church'
(op. cit., p. 81). The Spirit is no longer the eschatological
gift, but the power which permits the existence of believers in a continuing world and makes possible the
work of evangelism. It is for this reason that Luke embarks upon his historical work, in which he describes the
Church, its mission, and its relation to the world. In a
word, Luke historicizes the primitive eschatology; he was
compelled to do so by the fact that history was manifestly continuing, and thereby demonstrating that the
earliest believers were wrong in thinking the *parousia* to
be chronologically near. Luke dealt with the problem of
the 'delay of the *parousia*' by setting forth his conception
of a *Heilsgeschichte* ordered according to God's will in
continuous sec̶   ̶i̶d̶d̶l̶e̶ ̶o̶f̶ ̶w̶h̶i̶c̶h̶ ̶s̶t̶o̶o̶d̶ ̶the
time of
de
H

which moves continuously from creation to *parousia* through three epochs:

The time of Israel, of the law and the prophets.
The time of Jesus, as a preliminary manifestation of the coming salvation.
The time between Jesus' ministry and His *parousia*, the time, that is, of the Church, of the Spirit. This is the last age; Luke does not say that it will be short (op. cit., p. 129).

It is on these grounds, not simply in order to meet a practical need (such as Paul's defence before Caesar), that the Lucan apologetic arises. The fact that the time of the Church can no longer be disregarded as infinitesimally short makes it imperative for Christians to work out their relations with both Judaism and the State. Luke's own political attitude may summed up as follows (op. cit., p. 127):

(*a*) Over against the Jews: one must obey God rather than man;
(*b*) Over against the Empire: one must give to Caesar what is Caesar's, to God what is God's.

Jesus, as we have seen, stands in the middle of time. This raises the question of Christology: Who was Jesus Christ? Luke has no explicit pronouncement on the relation between the Father and the Son, but this is indirectly disclosed in several ways. Thus God alone is the agent of creation—no pre-existent Son is mentioned beside Him. The plan of salvation is exclusively *God's* plan. In it Jesus acts as God's instrument, and does so not in virtue of metaphysical or essential unity with God, but because God anoints Him, and equips Him with the necessary gifts and authority. These facts point clearly to a doctrine of subordinationism, 'which springs out of the tradition and fits smoothly into the Lucan *Historismus*'

(op. cit., pp. 159f.). At the same time, from the standpoint of the Church the work of Jesus appears to be
in full unity with that of the Father, so that Jesus is
rightly described as the *Lord*. Here, however, distinctions have to be made. Jesus was Lord (for example,
over demons) in the time of His ministry; He is Lord in
a different sense now that He reigns in heaven. He is
Lord over the Church, but not in quite the same sense
Lord over the world. We may quote Dr Conzelmann's
own summary of the position, and so pass to the last
section of his book (op. cit., p. 180):

The Lord is now in heaven. But the fellowship of the Church
lives on earth, equipped with the Spirit, provided with the
message, which is communicated through witnesses, and with
the regular operation of the sacraments. The Church is not
created by the resurrection (it is created by God, not by an
independently operative 'saving event' as such; with Luke
we have not yet got so far as that); but the presupposition of
the Church's existence is fulfilled by the resurrection. The
next event in the series of saving acts is no longer concerned
with the story (*Weg*) of Jesus (and only thereby with the
Church), but with the Church direct: the out-pouring of the
Spirit. We turn to the conception of the Church and of
the means by which salvation is appropriated.

It is the Church that must be studied, for Luke does
not concern himself with the place of the individual in
the *Heilsgeschichte*; the individual is incorporated into the
Church and thereby stands in appropriate relation to
the divine purpose. It is this continuing function of the
Church that robs of its importance the lengthening interval between the time of Jesus and the *parousia*; it is through
the Church and its ministrations that the Spirit is be-
stowed.

Within the time of the Church as a whole the earliest
period has unique significance, because it is the time of

the witnesses; hence the importance to Luke of describing the earliest community. In this description two lines cross, for Luke wishes to depict the Church as living in the midst of persecution, yet also as flourishing in peace. This dialectic can be traced not only in the story of the Jerusalem church, but also in the account of Paul. The Church inherits the place of Israel; because it also inherits the Old Testament Scriptures it finds itself obliged to prosecute a world-wide missionary task, for which it is equipped by the Spirit. In this activity God Himself is the primary subject, but this fact is sometimes veiled by a tendency to regard events as complete in themselves, and as human acts which only by an afterthought are ascribed to God. Luke knows that he is describing a unique period, in which the apostolic witnesses appear as no more than commissioned messengers, speaking not their own message but God's word. This emphasis accounts for the fact that Luke has so little to say about the later conception of Church officials. He knows that there are such persons, and names familiar in later use occasionally appear (Acts 20[28]; 11[30]; 14[23]; etc.). The ministers of Luke's own day are connected with the apostolic age not by a succession but by the Spirit.

Luke adds no speculative elements to the Christian proclamation, but his writing reveals a Christian vocabulary fast becoming technical. Acts shows a formulation of Christian confession, and the gospel the tradition about Jesus which constitutes the message. The Church has not yet become part of its own message, though Luke prepares for this later stage of proclamation by giving to the Church and its history a special place within the *Heilsgeschichte* as a whole.

Christian life both in its origin (conversion) and its continuance is given its form by the delay of the *parousia*. Great stress is laid on a strongly ethical conception of sin, repentance, and forgiveness. Life is a future gift, but because it is guaranteed by the Spirit it is no longer dependent on the nearness of the kingdom of God. Christian baptism comes to be more and more separated from John's baptism, and closely connected with the Spirit. So with the Christian life beyond baptism:

The postponement of the eschatology results *eo ipso* in a structural change in ethical thought. Out of existence in the eschatological community with its expectation of a near end there now emerges the *vita Christiana*. The judgement remains a motive, no longer, however, on account of its nearness but simply as a fact. The real problems, which Luke prefers to handle, are those which arise out of the situation of the Church in the continuing world. Along with the shaping of everyday life goes especially the question of the Christian's attitude under persecution (op. cit., p. 204).

6. The most considerable commentary on Acts written in recent years is that of Dr Ernst Haenchen.[44] Its qualities as an exposition of the text must here be left out of account; we shall concentrate upon Dr Haenchen's views of Luke's purpose and methods. In his Introduction he provides (op. cit., pp. 13-47) an admirable survey of the historical and critical study of Acts. There is much information here, and there are many suggestive observations, which we must be content to pass by, though it might have been both interesting and instructive to note the impression made upon this widely read German scholar by modern English work on Acts. Dr Haenchen deplores the lack of any history of the study of Acts corresponding to Dr Albert Schweitzer's *The Quest of the Historical Jesus*, and *Paul and his Interpreters*; he has himself done as much as space permitted to remedy the deficiency.

Dr Haenchen's own views (so far as they touch our

[44] *Die Apostelgeschichte* ("Kritisch-Exegetischer Kommentar über das Neue Testament," 3; fourteenth edition, fifth of Haenchen's commentary [Göttingen, 1965]).

Why does Luke choose to build up his artistic work on this principle of two-foldness (varied occasionally by three-foldness)? The answer is given in Dr Morgenthaler's second volume, in the observation that Luke intends by means of his work to bear witness, and it is laid down in Scripture (Deut. 19[15]; cf. Matt. 18[16ff.]; 2 Cor. 13[1]; 1 Tim. 5[19]; Heb. 10[28]; 1 John 5[6ff.]) that testimony is to be received *at the mouth of two or three witnesses*.[40] Hence Luke's tautologies, doublets, and repetitions. And, more important, hence also a vindication of Luke's character as a historian. The trustworthiness of the Lucan histories has been attacked, according to Dr Morgenthaler, on two main lines, which he neatly, and not inaccurately, summarizes thus (op. cit., ii, p. 25):

1. Luke's historical writing is a work of art, but is not truly historical; for art has to do with aesthetics, and has nothing at all to do with crude historicity.
2. Luke's historical writing is testimony, but is by no means truly historical; for testimony has to do with theology, and has nothing at all to do with crude historicity.

But Luke's art is the art of two-foldness (and three-foldness), and this shows that the only kind of testimony Luke means to offer is that which would satisfy a law-court, which demands twofold and threefold testimony. Luke is narrating a redemptive history (*Heilsgeschichte*), and this means that he is speaking of a historical (*geschichtlich*) redemption. This observation is more important than comparisons between Luke and other ancient historians.[41] Luke was well equipped to write history, and the form his history took arose not out of his imagination

[40] On this theme see H. van Vliet, *No Single Testimony* (Utrecht, 1958), especially n. 19.

[41] Cf. below, p. 61. It would not, however, follow from this observation that the examination of historical models is valueless in the study of Acts.

but out of the historical event itself. Dr Morgenthaler applies to Luke's work as a whole words written by Schlatter with reference to Luke 1 (op. cit., ii, p. 110): 'This narrative has often been called a poem. Were that the whole truth, he who wrote it would be among the greatest who ever received the poetic gift. But there is divine poetry as well as human; and more poetic than all poetry is the history which the Spirit of God brings about.'

5. Another book that deals with the Lucan writings as a whole is Dr Hans Conzelmann's *Die Mitte der Zeit*,[42] a book which must be regarded as the outstanding modern assessment of Lucan theology. It falls into five parts, of which the first is the hardest to summarize, for in it Dr Conzelmann surveys rapidly the gospel material as a whole, treating each pericope or larger unit in turn and assessing its significance for his inquiry into Luke's theological presuppositions, methods, and results. Here we must be content with a few illustrative examples. Dr Conzelmann deals first with John the Baptist. Except in the nativity stories Luke recognizes no typological correspondence between John and Jesus. John does not appear as a forerunner, as Elijah, or as a sign of the advent. He is a prophet, a preacher of repentance, and thus a representative of the former age. In him and Jesus two periods in the one history of redemption (*Heilsgeschichte*) come together at their common boundary; but the two men stand on opposite sides of the frontier. It is John's work and not his person that prepares the way for Jesus. 'In this way John acquires a clearly defined function in the *middle* of the *Heilsgeschichte*. If it is his ministry, not his existence, that is the preparation for Jesus, then he is subordinated to the work of Jesus in the same way

42 Tübingen, 1954; revised edition, 1960. An English translation has been published during the writing of this lecture: *The Theology of St Luke* (London, 1960).

as the whole epoch of the Law' (op. cit., p. 15). For example, his death is the death of a prophet, not an eschatological event (cf. Luke 9⁹ with Mark 9¹²ᶠ·).

Dr Conzelmann's treatment of the ministry of Jesus himself may be represented by his discussion of a characteristic passage, Luke 4¹⁶⁻³⁰.

The theme Promise-Fulfilment is set forth by means of two biblical quotations. The first, in vv. 18f., expressly announces fulfilment in the 'Present'. Schlatter (221)[43] describes its content thus: 'What Jesus said to the men of Nazareth was the Gospel, without veil. He brings them the time of salvation (*Heilszeit*).' One recalls 2 Cor. 6²: ἰδοὺ νῦν καιρὸς εὐπρόσδεκτός. But when Luke makes Jesus say: σήμερον πεπλήρωται ἡ γραφὴ αὕτη, the distinction becomes clear: Paul describes his *own* as the eschatological time, but Luke sees salvation already in the past. The time of salvation has become historic, a period of time which certainly determines the present, but as an epoch is past and closed. That Luke is clear about this matter is shown by the analogous paragraph 22³⁵ᶠ·, which sets over against each other the time of Jesus and the present. This signifies neither more nor less than the conception that the time of the End (*Endzeit*) did not break in with Jesus. Rather, the future time of salvation was portrayed in advance in the middle of the *Heilsgeschichte* in the life of Jesus. This is a portrayal which even now establishes our hope; more, it is an event which gives us forgiveness and the Spirit, and thereby entry into the future salvation. But this does not alter the fact that the time of Jesus, like the present, is not yet the *last* time. The good news is not that the kingdom of God has come, but that through the life of Jesus the hope of the coming kingdom has been established. Its nearness thus becomes a secondary factor (op. cit., p. 27).

These observations are fundamental to Dr Conzelmann's thesis, and lead naturally to a discussion of the

[43] The reference is to A. Schlatter, *Das Evangelium des Lukas aus seinen Quellen erklärt* (Stuttgart, 1931).

Lucan eschatology. If we wish to understand Luke's own eschatological thinking (as distinct from that of Jesus or of the earliest Church), what we must look for is tension or discrepancy between his sources and his editing of them. An example may be found in the quotation from Joel in Acts 2[17ff.]. Naturally, Luke as well as his source takes the quotation to mean that the gift of the Spirit is a sign of the last time, but whereas for the source, the 'last days' are truly the End, for Luke himself they stretch out into a continuous tract of history, so that 'the outpouring of the Spirit is no longer in itself the *Eschaton*, but the opening of a lengthy epoch, the time of the Church' (op. cit., p. 81). The Spirit is no longer the eschatological gift, but the power which permits the existence of believers in a continuing world and makes possible the work of evangelism. It is for this reason that Luke embarks upon his historical work, in which he describes the Church, its mission, and its relation to the world. In a word, Luke historicizes the primitive eschatology; he was compelled to do so by the fact that history was manifestly continuing, and thereby demonstrating that the earliest believers were wrong in thinking the *parousia* to be chronologically near. Luke dealt with the problem of the 'delay of the *parousia*' by setting forth his conception of a *Heilsgeschichte* ordered according to God's will in continuous sections, in the middle of which stood the time of Jesus. The next epoch, that of the Church, is determined by Jesus Christ Himself and by the Spirit. Hence follow Dr Conzelmann's next subjects of discussion—Christian existence in the world, Christology, and the Church.

Christians exist in history in relation to Judaism, and to the political authority. It is consideration of these two factors that leads Luke to apologetics. The position of the Church in the world is determined by the *Heilsgeschichte* which moves continuously from creation to *parousia* through three epochs:

The time of Israel, of the law and the prophets.
The time of Jesus, as a preliminary manifestation of the coming salvation.
The time between Jesus' ministry and His *parousia*, the time, that is, of the Church, of the Spirit. This is the last age; Luke does not say that it will be short (op. cit., p. 129).

It is on these grounds, not simply in order to meet a practical need (such as Paul's defence before Caesar), that the Lucan apologetic arises. The fact that the time of the Church can no longer be disregarded as infinitesimally short makes it imperative for Christians to work out their relations with both Judaism and the State. Luke's own political attitude may summed up as follows (op. cit., p. 127):

(*a*) Over against the Jews: one must obey God rather than man;
(*b*) Over against the Empire: one must give to Caesar what is Caesar's, to God what is God's.

Jesus, as we have seen, stands in the middle of time. This raises the question of Christology: Who was Jesus Christ? Luke has no explicit pronouncement on the relation between the Father and the Son, but this is indirectly disclosed in several ways. Thus God alone is the agent of creation—no pre-existent Son is mentioned beside Him. The plan of salvation is exclusively *God's* plan. In it Jesus acts as God's instrument, and does so not in virtue of metaphysical or essential unity with God, but because God anoints Him, and equips Him with the necessary gifts and authority. These facts point clearly to a doctrine of subordinationism, 'which springs out of the tradition and fits smoothly into the Lucan *Historismus*'

(op. cit., pp. 159f.). At the same time, from the standpoint of the Church the work of Jesus appears to be
in full unity with that of the Father, so that Jesus is
rightly described as the *Lord*. Here, however, distinctions have to be made. Jesus was Lord (for example,
over demons) in the time of His ministry; He is Lord in
a different sense now that He reigns in heaven. He is
Lord over the Church, but not in quite the same sense
Lord over the world. We may quote Dr Conzelmann's
own summary of the position, and so pass to the last
section of his book (op. cit., p. 180):

The Lord is now in heaven. But the fellowship of the Church
lives on earth, equipped with the Spirit, provided with the
message, which is communicated through witnesses, and with
the regular operation of the sacraments. The Church is not
created by the resurrection (it is created by God, not by an
independently operative 'saving event' as such; with Luke
we have not yet got so far as that); but the presupposition of
the Church's existence is fulfilled by the resurrection. The
next event in the series of saving acts is no longer concerned
with the story (*Weg*) of Jesus (and only thereby with the
Church), but with the Church direct: the out-pouring of the
Spirit. We turn to the conception of the Church and of
the means by which salvation is appropriated.

It is the Church that must be studied, for Luke does
not concern himself with the place of the individual in
the *Heilsgeschichte*; the individual is incorporated into the
Church and thereby stands in appropriate relation to
the divine purpose. It is this continuing function of the
Church that robs of its importance the lengthening interval between the time of Jesus and the *parousia*; it is through
the Church and its ministrations that the Spirit is be-
stowed.

Within the time of the Church as a whole the earliest
period has unique significance, because it is the time of

the witnesses; hence the importance to Luke of describing the earliest community. In this description two lines cross, for Luke wishes to depict the Church as living in the midst of persecution, yet also as flourishing in peace. This dialectic can be traced not only in the story of the Jerusalem church, but also in the account of Paul. The Church inherits the place of Israel; because it also inherits the Old Testament Scriptures it finds itself obliged to prosecute a world-wide missionary task, for which it is equipped by the Spirit. In this activity God Himself is the primary subject, but this fact is sometimes veiled by a tendency to regard events as complete in themselves, and as human acts which only by an afterthought are ascribed to God. Luke knows that he is describing a unique period, in which the apostolic witnesses appear as no more than commissioned messengers, speaking not their own message but God's word. This emphasis accounts for the fact that Luke has so little to say about the later conception of Church officials. He knows that there are such persons, and names familiar in later use occasionally appear (Acts 20[28]; 11[30]; 14[23]; etc.). The ministers of Luke's own day are connected with the apostolic age not by a succession but by the Spirit.

Luke adds no speculative elements to the Christian proclamation, but his writing reveals a Christian vocabulary fast becoming technical. Acts shows a formulation of Christian confession, and the gospel the tradition about Jesus which constitutes the message. The Church has not yet become part of its own message, though Luke prepares for this later stage of proclamation by giving to the Church and its history a special place within the *Heilsgeschichte* as a whole.

Christian life both in its origin (conversion) and its continuance is given its form by the delay of the *parousia*. Great stress is laid on a strongly ethical conception of sin, repentance, and forgiveness. Life is a future gift, but because it is guaranteed by the Spirit it is no longer dependent on the nearness of the kingdom of God. Christian baptism comes to be more and more separated from John's baptism, and closely connected with the Spirit. So with the Christian life beyond baptism:

The postponement of the eschatology results *eo ipso* in a structural change in ethical thought. Out of existence in the eschatological community with its expectation of a near end there now emerges the *vita Christiana*. The judgement remains a motive, no longer, however, on account of its nearness but simply as a fact. The real problems, which Luke prefers to handle, are those which arise out of the situation of the Church in the continuing world. Along with the shaping of everyday life goes especially the question of the Christian's attitude under persecution (op. cit., p. 204).

6. The most considerable commentary on Acts written in recent years is that of Dr Ernst Haenchen.[44] Its qualities as an exposition of the text must here be left out of account; we shall concentrate upon Dr Haenchen's views of Luke's purpose and methods. In his Introduction he provides (op. cit., pp. 13-47) an admirable survey of the historical and critical study of Acts. There is much information here, and there are many suggestive observations, which we must be content to pass by, though it might have been both interesting and instructive to note the impression made upon this widely read German scholar by modern English work on Acts. Dr Haenchen deplores the lack of any history of the study of Acts corresponding to Dr Albert Schweitzer's *The Quest of the Historical Jesus*, and *Paul and his Interpreters*; he has himself done as much as space permitted to remedy the deficiency.

Dr Haenchen's own views (so far as they touch our

[44] *Die Apostelgeschichte* ("Kritisch-Exegetischer Kommentar über das Neue Testament," 3; fourteenth edition, fifth of Haenchen's commentary [Göttingen, 1965]).

present interests) are summed up in a chapter (op. cit., pp. 81-99) headed 'Luke as Theologian, Historian, and Author'. The three themes suggested by this title are treated in succession, though Dr Haenchen begins by pointing out that, with Luke, theology, history, and authorship are closely bound up together. It is because of his theology that Luke was driven to interest himself in, and to write, history.

We begin, however, with theology. Luke was no systematic theologian, and his theological presuppositions are simple. On the doctrines of God the Father and of Jesus Christ, Dr Haenchen acknowledges that he has little to add to the work done by Dr Conzelmann. God the Father is the author of creation, and of salvation. We hear nothing of the pre-existence of Christ, and there is the barest hint (Acts 20[28]) of an atoning death. Jesus sends the Spirit, because it has been granted to Him by the Father to do so. There is no suggestion of the later doctrine of the Trinity. There is no developed doctrine of the Church; only at Acts 9[31] does the word ἐκκλησία mean more than 'local community'. The first bearers of the Word of God are the twelve apostles, but these disappear without any assertion of an apostolic succession. Paul takes over the work of the Gentile mission in virtue of his special call, and when he and Silas appoint elders, these are authorized by the Holy Spirit to lead the communities; there is still no ground for speaking of apostolic succession. Conversion means repentance, turning to God, faith in Christ; these are the conditions for baptism, in which the Spirit is conferred. There are allusions to the Lord's Supper, but no sacramental piety of the Ignatian kind. 'This, with many other things, shows that one must be cautious in using the term "*Frühkatholizismus*" (primitive catholicism)' (op. cit., p. 84).[45]

---

[45] See above, p. 25, and below, pp. 70-6, with the references, especially to E. Käsemann.

Two theological concerns of Luke's own day are in evidence: (1) the nearness of the End, and (2) the freedom of the Gentile mission from the law. The second of these arises more naturally in the discussion of Luke as a historian. The first is treated under the head of theology. The earliest Christians believed that they were already living in the last days, which had been inaugurated by the resurrection of Jesus. Little time remained before His *parousia*, and in this short interval the good news must be spread as far as possible, so that faith in Jesus might save men in the imminent judgement. When this hope of an early *parousia* was disappointed, two courses were open. To the Fourth Evangelist, the last events—judgement and the gift of eternal life—were brought into the present, being realized in the present hearing of the Word of God. This was not Luke's answer. He took more seriously than John the chronological extension of time before the *parousia*, and in view of it developed a new doctrine of the *Heilsgeschichte*. In expounding this, Dr Haenchen agrees closely with Dr Conzelmann.[46] The time of Jesus belongs to the past, not to the present; hence Luke must write as a historian, and 'his gospel is the first "Life of Jesus" ' (op. cit., p. 87).[47] Hence also the plan of Acts. The time of Jesus is the time of salvation; after this period, there remains the dissemination of the Word of God—which is the bearer and agent of salvation—through the whole world. This task is completed in representative fashion when

[46] See above, pp. 40-6.

[47] Haenchen here refers to E. Käsemann's very important essay, long too little known, "The Problem of the Historical Jesus," originally in *ZThK*, li (1954), pp. 125-53, reprinted in *Ex. Ver. I* (see above, p. 7, n. 2), pp. 187–214; Eng. trans. by W. J. Montague, in Käsemann's *Essays on New Testament Themes* ("Studies in Biblical Theology," 41; London, 1964), pp. 15-47. Eng. trans., p. 29: "His Gospel is indeed the first 'life of Jesus'. In it, consideration is given to the points of view of causality and teleology; and psychological insight, the comparison of the historian and the particular slant of the writer who aims at edification are all equally discernible."

Paul reaches Rome, and at this point accordingly the story of Acts breaks off.

Luke's task as a historian is to show how the founding of the Jewish church in Jerusalem led to the universal Gentile mission, and did so without contradicting that continuity between Israel and the Church which marks the *Heilsgeschichte*. Luke's answer to this problem is: 'Those who founded and conducted the Christian mission did not fall away from their Jewish faith; rather, they kept it faithfully. But God led them, unmistakably and irresistibly, to the Gentile mission' (op. cit., p. 90). Thus Luke is able to smooth over the conflicts which arose in the early Church, and to claim and illustrate the protection to which it was entitled (as being the genuine Judiasm) from the Roman authorities. For this straightforward and superficially satisfying account, however, Luke as a historian had to pay a heavy price, of which Dr Haenchen gives two examples. (1) In truth, it was not the apostles but Stephen and the Hellenists who initiated the Gentile mission; (2) Luke's picture of Paul is demonstrably unhistorical. That is, in order to safeguard the theological continuity of the *Heilsgeschichte*, Luke departs significantly from history 'as it really happened'.

Luke was no Thucydides, nor even a Xenophon. For such a role he lacked both the historical material, and the readers. His clientele were not interested in scientific history. Luke worked up the several narratives of his book with an eye to their practical effectiveness. In illustration of this assertion, Dr Haenchen discusses the appointment of Matthias, the arrest of Paul, his appearance before Festus and Agrippa, and his conversion.

Luke's conception of a narrator's vocation was evidently different from ours. It was not necessary to describe an event

D

with the exactness of a police report, but to bring what happened to the consciousness of the hearer or reader in its inner significance, and to impress upon the reader unforgettably the truth of the power of God expressed in the event. The obedience of the author finds its fulfilment precisely in the freedom of his rendering (op. cit., p. 99).

It must be evident that the space that remains for the third part of this lecture will not allow either a detailed criticism of the views that have now been summarily set forth, or a general treatment of the problems raised by the Lucan literature. Only a few brief comments can be made; yet it seems desirable to draw the discussion together with an attempt at least to ask some of the right questions, and if possible to suggest a few answers which shall not be seriously misleading. This is no unimportant task. A generation ago, in his inaugural lecture at Cambridge,[48] Professor Dodd could claim that the Fourth Gospel constituted the most acute and pressing problem in New Testament studies. If this is less true today, the change is due to a great extent to Professor Dodd's own labour and scholarship. It would not be far wrong to say that the focus of New Testament studies is now moving to the Lucan writings. The Fourth Gospel raised, in one form, the problem which is always pressed upon the Christian thinker by the nature of his subject, namely, that of the relation between history and theology. It is the same ultimate problem that the Lucan writings raise, though they raise it in a different way.

That recent years have witnessed a revolution in Lucan studies, and that the changes involved have led to a more positive understanding of Luke's work, can scarcely be doubted. The six authors whose contributions have been summarized do not speak with one voice; indeed, we can safely leave them with little direct comment because they

[48] *The Present Task in New Testament Studies* (Cambridge, 1936).

comment on and dispute with one another. Yet when they are compared with New Testament critics of an earlier generation they are seen at once to share a common approach. They have abandoned the old search for literary sources, and think of Luke as an author, handling some literary material, perhaps, but himself responsible for collecting, digesting, and setting out information drawn from traditional and other sources. They recognize in Luke one of the New Testament preachers; no Paul, and no John, in his manner, yet a fellow-preacher with them. They recognize that Luke's vocation as a historian did not arise out of idle curiosity, but was (humanly speaking) forced upon him by the theological and ecclesiastical environment in which he lived. They recognize that, as a historian, Luke stands in the midst of a diverse group of historians of various races and styles. We may sum the matter up by saying that our survey of recent writers justifies the selection of the six questions which were raised in the first part of this lecture. The Lucan writings summon us to the study of ancient historiography of all kinds, and invite our inquiry into the Christian milieu in which they took shape.

How then are the Lucan writings to be assessed? Before they can be assessed at all we must know to what category of literature they belong. A volume of sermons (even though abounding in historical illustrations) must not be judged as if it were a collection of historical essays; a collection of historical essays (even though the author has not scrupled to point out 'morals') cannot be judged as if it were a volume of sermons. What sort of judgement does Luke invite us to pass on his book? If it is to be judged as fundamentally a historical work, whether a continuous narrative or a set of biographical sketches, then the question that must be asked (if we exclude purely artistic issues) is whether Luke gives us the story of events

'as they actually happened'. Does he put the right people
in the right places at the right times? Does he represent
accurately not only their deeds and words but also their
motives and intentions? Does he give the right connec-
tions between events? If, however, the Lucan literature
is more accurately described as preaching, if it was Luke's
intention to set out the substratum of Christian proclamation in the life and teaching of Jesus, and to illustrate
the proclamation itself in a series of classical models,
claimed and demonstrated as classical by being put in
the mouth of apostles and set in the context of the early
Church, then we must apply something like Luther's test
of apostolicity,[49] and inquire whether this literature
preaches Christ, and estimate its success in terms of the
clarity and power with which it bears witness to the central
figure. Which alternative is correct? Are we to base our
critical appraisal on historical or kerygmatic grounds?

I have put the question in this simple alternative form
only in order to reject it; for though the distinction it ex-
presses is familiar enough to us, it is one that Luke would
not have understood. Neither the history of Jesus, nor
that of the primitive Church, could be, in his mind,
divorced from preaching. Not that he is likely consciously
to have said to himself, 'I will preach Christ by writing
a gospel and the history of the apostolic age.' Even
though Luke is of all New Testament writers the most
self-conscious author, we must recognize that in writing
he was moved in the main by motives of which he was

---

[49] It may be interesting to quote part of Luther's (1533) Preface to Acts:
'Dies Buch soll man lesen und ansehen, nicht wie wir etwa gethan haben,
als hätte S. Lukas darin allein die eigenen persönlichen Werke oder
Geschichten der Apostel geschrieben, zum Exempel guter Werke oder
gutes Lebens. . . . Sondern darauf soll man merken, dass S. Lukas mit
diesem Buch die ganze Christenheit lehret, bis an der Welt Ende, das
rechte Hauptstück christlicher Lehre, nämlich, wie wir alle müssen gerecht
werden allein durch den Glauben an Jesum Christum, ohn alles Zutun
des Gesetzes oder Hülfe unser Werke.'

himself (in all probability) imperfectly aware. That he had in his make-up something of the story-teller, and that this gift had been fostered by some acquaintance with the romantic and historical literature of the Hellenistic age, need not be doubted; nor need it be doubted that he was an honest man, who would not in cold blood distort the truth or say that things had happened when he knew that they had not happened; nor that he admired the great apostles, especially Paul; nor that he was a sincere Christian, who accepted the authority, and wished to proclaim the redemptive work, of Jesus Christ. All these qualifications and motives contributed to his work, but they do not explain it. More important is the fact that the Church in Luke's day had reached a point at which a variety of considerations, some of which will be mentioned below, called for the sort of book Luke wrote, and that Luke became, as it were, the vehicle of the spirit of the age. There is a more theological and, ultimately, truer and more satisfying, way of putting the matter; but for the present this will do.

Luke's is a two-volume work. This observation, naïvely simple at first sight, is of great importance, and marks Luke off from all other New Testament writers, and Luke-Acts from all other New Testament books. These all stand on one side or other of a great watershed. They are aware of it; they presuppose its existence; but they do not describe it, and they show little explicit interest in that which lies on the side of it which they are not handling. Mark, for example, tells the story of the ministry of Jesus as the record of God's final dealings with mankind. The gospel begins (1^{15}) with the proclamation: The time is up; the kingdom of God is at hand. As the story continues it becomes clearer that the crisis of history lies ahead, but only just ahead. The Son of Man is about to suffer, and to give His life as a ransom (8^{31};

10^{45}). Beyond His death lies a divine act of vindication, of which there are two aspects, a rising out of the tomb and an appearing in heavenly glory. Mark knew that these two 'aspects' were in truth two events, separated from each other by an interval in time. He knew this, because he himself lived in the interval. But the time could not be long. His own generation would not disappear before the goal had been reached (9^1; 13^{30}). Not to 'you' (the apostles) only but to 'all' (Mark and his contemporaries), Jesus says: Watch (13^{37}). Tell the story of Jesus—His miracles, in which He overcame the mighty enemy of mankind; His parables, in which He disclosed the hidden connection between His humble life and the glorious harvest-home of the kingdom; His death and resurrection, the most wonderful miracle and the most secret parable of all—and you have told the story of God's act of redemption, so that any postscript must seem the merest anti-climax.

Mark represents one kind of New Testament writing. For Paul, the story begins where Mark ends. For him too, Jesus is Christ crucified and risen; but only once does he look behind the crucifixion to an event in the ministry of Jesus, and then only so far as to the night in which Jesus was betrayed, and in order to interpret the rite in which the Church of his own day recalled the death of Jesus and looked forward to His return. The gospel tradition might not exist for all the use Paul makes of it in his letters. True, he never questions the historical existence of Jesus—if Jesus had not lived He could not have died; but Paul did not wish to tell stories about Him or to recount His teaching. And for good reason: Jesus was not a dead man of the past; He was alive, and reigning in heaven as the Lord, governing His people on earth through the Holy Spirit. There was no need to look into the past for His activity; it was to be seen in every stage of the Christian mission, as the Gospel had swept on its way from Jerusalem to Illyricum.

Mark, then, has at most hints[50] of what the future life of the Church will be: You shall be hated by all men for my sake (13¹³). Paul has at most hints of what the 'historical Jesus' was like: I beseech you by the meekness and gentleness of Christ (2 Cor. 10¹). That is, neither Mark nor Paul can be said to explain or even to describe the relation between the 'Jesus of history' and the Church. That they believed in a connection between the two is certain, but neither had occasion to demonstrate or discuss it. Luke, however, was compelled by the shape of his two-volume book, and by its subject-matter, to deal with precisely this question. He is the only New Testament writer who makes any conscious attempt to show how, when the earthly life of Jesus was over, the Church came into being, and to relate the one to the other.[51] This fact not only makes Luke a fascinating figure to modern students; it supplied him with his motive for writing, and provides the clue to his work.

That Luke was aware that he was building a bridge between two periods appears from the fact that his two volumes overlap, the crucial material about the resurrection and the ascension being given twice,[52] once in Luke 24 and once in Acts 1. Acts 1³⁻⁸ briefly repeats and summarizes the resurrection appearances; for example, συναλιζόμενος ('eating together with') in 1⁴ takes up the meal at Emmaus and the eating of fish at Luke 24⁴¹ᶠᶠ.

[50] This statement is not intended to deny that the whole of Mark was written with a view to the needs and circumstances of the Church; but these needs and circumstances must be sought beneath the surface of the narrative.

[51] It is from this fact that the unique importance of Luke in modern *Leben-Jesu-Forschung* arises.

[52] I am here indebted to the important observations of P. A. van Stempvoort, 'The Interpretation of the Ascension in Luke and Acts', *New Testament Studies*, v (1958), pp. 30-42.

Even more important is the repetition of the ascension narrative. In asserting this repetition we are not dependent on the Western Non-Interpolation of Luke 24⁵¹ (καὶ ἀνεφέρετο εἰς τὸν οὐρανόν), though this should probably be accepted as the correct reading.⁵³ Even without these words the text describes a parting between Jesus and His disciples so decisive that one cannot but be surprised to find them together again, and to read a second account (Acts 1⁹ᶠᶠ·) of their separation. It is true that a writer may summarize a preceding volume at the beginning of the next, but though this might account for the summary repetition of the resurrection appearances, it cannot explain the fact that in Acts the ascension is recounted *de novo*. The explanation is that the ascension is not one event but two; or, rather, it is one event which bears different appearances, when looked at from different angles. On the one hand, the ascension is the end of the story of Jesus, who works cures, perishes in Jerusalem, and on the third day is perfected (cf. Luke 13³²). All the essential events are crowded into this third day, on which Jesus rises from the dead, walks to Emmaus, appears to Simon, and in the midst of the disciples, eats in their presence, explains the Scriptures to them, and bids them await the Holy Spirit. He has fulfilled prophecy, carried out to the full the work of obedience, and triumphed over death. It remains for Him only to take His place in heaven. On the other hand, the ascension is the beginning of the story of the Church. It is from this viewpoint that we see it in Acts. It is preceded by a verse (1⁸) which predicts the world-wide mission of the Church (cf. Luke 24⁴⁷). Afterwards, those who have taken part wait for the next chapter in the

---

⁵³ See (in addition to the commentaries) the discussion of Western omissions in Luke by J. Jeremias, *The Eucharistic Words of Jesus*, rev. ed., trans. by N. Perrin (New York, 1966), pp. 145-52.

story to begin. It is particularly important that the angelic attendants (1^{10}) point forward from the ascension to the *parousia*, of which there is no hint in the gospel narrative. There, the ascension closes an epoch; here, it opens another, which will last until it ends with the return of Christ from heaven, where in the meantime He sits at God's right hand (Acts $2^{33f.}$; 5^{31}; $7^{55f.}$) as the Lord who through His Spirit directs the work of His Church on earth.

Out of Luke's double understanding of the ascension arises a second double proposition of even greater importance. Since the ascension is for Luke both the end of the ministry of Jesus, in which His life finds the triumphant conclusion that gives it meaning, and the beginning of the Church, which makes the life of the Church both possible and intelligible, it follows that, in Luke's thought, the end of the story of Jesus is the Church; and, the story of Jesus is the beginning of the Church. In this proposition lie the distinctive characteristics of Luke's work. He shares with Mark and Paul the conviction that Jesus is the End,[54] God's final word and deed; but when his work is compared with theirs, the reader finds himself asking, What does 'the End' mean? For every New Testament writer, the time that falls after the resurrection, whether long or short, is the last chapter in history. For Mark and Paul, the stress lies on the adjective *last*. For Luke, the stress lies on the fact that the last chapter is a *new* chapter. Christ is the End; but (and this is how Luke prefers to think of Him) because He is the End He is also the Beginning. He is not the close of all history, but the starting-point of a new kind of history, Church History, whose horizons are indefinitely remote. This is what Luke perceived, and this is

[54] I prefer this way of expressing the matter to Conzelmann's (cf. p. 41 above), though without wishing to express anything radically different.

what gives him his unique place in the New Testament.
He is the Father of Church History; it had not occurred
to any Christian before him that there was any such
thing.[55] Once, however, Luke had conceived the notion
that the triumphant conclusion of the story of Jesus con-
tained the germ of a historical process which was to unfold
itself in the course of what he knew was already a fairly
considerable period, his vocation as a historian was determined. Indeed, it was determined not only that he
should write history, but also how he should write it.

In the first place, it was determined that he should
tell the story of Jesus as that of the founder of a religion.
It is in this respect that Luke's story differs in form and
outlook from those of the other three gospels. This
motive (together no doubt with Luke's religious and
literary background) accounts for the parallels noted at
an earlier point in this lecture[56] between the figure of
Jesus and that of the 'divine man' (θεῖος ἀνήρ). Luke
was interested in what may be called 'religious personalities'. His account of John the Baptist is characteristic.
He neither explicitly identifies the Baptist with Elijah, as
Matthew does (Matt. 11¹⁴), nor explicitly repudiates the
identification, as John does (John 1²¹), but claims that
the Baptist will go before his greater successor 'in the
spirit and power of Elijah' (Luke 1¹⁷); that is, he, like
Elijah, will be a powerful prophetic preacher. Jesus is
such another. So, for that matter, are Peter, Stephen,
and Paul, and all of them are concerned in the foundation
of the new religious community, though Luke never
wavers in the conviction that among them all Jesus is
unique. He is, however, unique not so much in the out-
ward pattern of His life (though it is always perfectly

[55] Cf. what was said on p. 27. Luke knew that he had predecessors when
he wrote a gospel; he refers to none for the writing of Church History.
[56] See pp. 12-15.

clear that He is the central figure, to whom all the rest
are subordinate) as in the fact that after His earthly
ministry He was exalted to heaven, there to rule at God's
right hand. In His ministry He does all that religious
leaders, the founders of religious schools, do. He teaches
admiring crowds, appoints disciples, sends them out to
prepare the way for Himself, confounds His adversaries,
resolves the difficulties of inquirers, and escapes unharmed
the machinations of His foes. If it is pointed out that
examples of all these activities can be found in the other
gospels, the reply is twofold. First, it is not disputed that
these stories are told elsewhere—it is in fact not difficult
to believe that such incidents actually took place; what
is distinctive is Luke's way of telling, and of assembling,
them. Secondly, in Luke the stress lies on these activities,
and not where Mark (for example) places it, on the death
of Jesus. Creed's saying on the absence from Luke of a
theologia crucis was referred to above.[57] We now see the
reason for the fact Creed noted (and possibly exaggerated).
Mark set forth in its full horror the paradox that the Son
of God died deserted even by His Father (15^{34}), and
asserts that in so dying Jesus gave His life as a ransom
for many (10^{45}). There is no ransom-saying, and there
is no cry of dereliction, in Luke. The 'happy ending'
never disappears, even at the worst moment. The reader
of 4^{16-30} knows[58] that Jesus is sure to escape, and that
His sufferings will have their fruit in the Church He
founds. It corresponds to this that in the sermons in
Acts the death of Christ tends to be treated negatively,
as an unfortunate event which nevertheless, in view of
the resurrection, need not be an obstacle to faith. Acts
20^{28} is a light weight to balance against the bulk of Luke's

[57] See p. 23; cf. Conzelmann, op. cit., p. 175, and Haenchen, referred
to on p. 47 above.
[58] See the discussion of the passage on pp. 64 f.

references to the Cross, which suggest not an atoning sacrifice but a temporary reverse, not unforeseen, and speedily retrieved.

The same conviction about the relation between Jesus and the Church determined, in the second place, the way in which Acts should be written. Luke had to write this book in such a way as to show that the story of the Church was not an independent or spontaneous movement, but the outcome of the life of Jesus. The speeches in Acts, by whomsoever made, all revert to the story of Jesus. This is never recounted—Luke was too economical an artist for this; but everywhere it is allusively present. Paul at Athens preached Jesus and the resurrection (Acts 17[18]); and it would scarcely exaggerate to say that these are the twin themes of all the sermons in Acts. The reason is clear. The speeches are the means Luke uses[59] to bring out the meaning of the history he narrates; and this is its meaning. It springs from the life of Jesus. Another feature of Acts that may be traced to the same source is the radical simplification of the narrative. The course of the Gentile mission, and the controversies it evoked, are pruned and curtailed, and appear in Acts only in the simplest outline, as if the Church had expanded from Jerusalem as concentric ripples spread across a pond from the place where a stone drops into it, and as if the only opposition to the inclusion of Gentiles arose from a few eccentric and ill-informed people, who were speedily put right. The truth is that the Gospel advanced by fits and starts, and in different directions moved at different speeds. The original Palestinian disciples were not the pioneers of its expansion but (if we may judge from the Pauline epistles) helped to constitute the op-

[59] Cf. Dibelius's account (p. 28 above) of the different kinds of insight which speeches may be used to give. His first and fourth points are relevant here.

position. This complicated and painful story Luke does not tell, partly perhaps because he did not know it, but partly also because, if he had told it, it would have obscured the connection between the story of Jesus and the story of the Church. He found it necessary to show that those who had been with Jesus in His ministry took the lead in the Gentile mission, because only in this way could he visibly connect the Gentile mission with Jesus.

It is this fundamental principle, rather than the influence of models whether Hellenistic or Jewish, that accounts for the way in which Luke set about the writing of history. Dr Ehrhardt's observation[60] is fundamentally correct: Luke's method is that of historical biography. He has no eye for social history,[61] and his crowd scenes are always dominated by a few individuals. The Acts of the Apostles is the story of Peter and of Paul, with Stephen, Philip, and James in supporting roles. In writing history by means of biography Luke was no innovator; nor need we look only to the Old Testament for parallels. Plutarch alone contributed not a few biographies to the Greek corpus, and many other relevant examples could be cited —beginning from Herodotus himself, who fills a much larger canvas than Luke's, but fills a good deal of it with biographical sketches. Luke, however, uses the biographical method not because there was good precedent for doing so, but because it suited his purpose. In the gospel his purpose was to tell the story of the Founder of the Church; this set the pattern for Acts, in which he showed how the Spirit of Jesus moulded men in His likeness, and used them in the continuation of His work. No other historical form would have made his point so clearly.

[60] See pp. 32f.
[61] His accounts of the social life of Christians are few and brief: Acts 2^{44-7}; 4^{32-5}; 6^1; 9^{39}; 11^{27-30}; $18^{2f.}$.

I have made the claim that it was Luke's perception that the development of the Church was germinally present in the victory of Jesus that led him to the writing of history; it is now necessary to dig more deeply into the roots of Luke's literary activity. What was it that put him in the way of this fruitful perception? He was led to it, under God, by the circumstances of his time and the practical necessities of the Church in his day. What were these circumstances and necessities? It is probable that Luke-Acts was written towards the close of the first century, probably not far from the date of the Fourth Gospel. It is likely that Luke and John were confronted by similar problems. The background of the Fourth Gospel, and the theological issues which the evangelist handled, I have discussed elsewhere,[62] and may here mention in all brevity the two outstanding problems of the day—the problem of gnosticism, and the problem of eschatology. Both Luke and John were obliged to deal with them, but they dealt with them in different ways.

John made a positive approach to gnosticism, using some of its language in order to destroy its errors.[63] This Luke did not do. His attitude is a direct negative. It may be that he pillories gnostic leaders in the person of Simon Magus (Acts 8[9-24]); it is certain that at a later time the figure of the Magus was regarded as the fountainhead of gnostic heresy, and Luke may already have looked upon him in this light, and intended his rebuke by Peter as an example to be followed by later Christian teachers. A more important observation, however, is that Luke studiously avoids gnostic thought and language. He

[62] *The Gospel according to St John* (London, 1955), especially pp. 22-33, 114-19.

[63] See my article, "The Theological Vocabulary of the Fourth Gospel and the Gospel of Truth," in *Current Issues in New Testament Interpretation: Essays in Honor of Otto A. Piper,* ed. W. Klassen and G. F. Snyder (New York, 1962), pp. 210-23, 297f.

shares the attitude of the Pastorals, though he is pre-
vented by his subject-matter[64] from uttering the explicit:
O Timothy, guard the deposit, and turn away from pro-
fane babblings, and the contradictions of falsely so-called
gnosis (1 Tim. 6[20]).

This comparison may take us a step further. It is not
only in regard to gnosticism that Acts resembles the
Pastorals; they agree also in their treatment of the figure
of Paul, which stood at the storm-centre of Judaism,
gnosticism, and orthodoxy.[65] For the author of the
Pastorals, as for Luke, Paul was a heroic character,
greatly admired, and perhaps less adequately understood.
Each was concerned to vindicate the hero, who was
heartily hated by Jewish (gnostic) Christians, and sus-
pected (as himself a gnostic) by some of the orthodox.
It is in this sense that Acts may be regarded as an apology
on behalf of Paul. It was not addressed to the Emperor,
with the intention of proving the political harmlessness
of Christianity in general and of Paul in particular; a
few passages might be construed to serve this purpose,
but to suggest that the book as a whole should be taken
in this way is absurd. No Roman official would ever
have filtered out so much of what to him would be theological and ecclesiastical rubbish in order to reach so tiny
a grain of relevant apology. So far as Acts was an apology, it was an apology addressed to the Church, demonstrating Paul's anti-gnostic orthodoxy, and his practical
and doctrinal solidarity with the church at Jerusalem.[66]

Luke, then, rejects gnosticism root and branch. His

[64] Cf., however, Acts 20[29f.]. Whatever source Luke may have used for
this address to the Ephesian elders he doubtless thought it applicable to
Christian ministers in his own day.

[65] Cf. C. K. Barrett, *The Pastoral Epistles in the New English Bible,
With Introduction and Commentary* ("The New Clarendon Bible"; Oxford, 1963).

[66] And, probably, making this solidarity appear much greater than in
fact it was.

attitude to the eschatological problem, that is, the grow-
ing inadequacy of eschatological language effectively to
express the Christian faith, is more subtle and important.
Out of the primitive Christian eschatology, which, so far
as it insisted upon an early *parousia* of the Son of man,
had proved mistaken and misleading, he evolved the
notion of *Heilsgeschichte*, a continuous historical process
which was the vehicle of God's saving purpose. Mark's
theological frame of reference led him to the meta-
historical categories and values of apocalyptic; Luke's led
him to the categories and values of history. It is for this
reason that the Third Gospel can be called the first 'Life
of Jesus'.[67] Two simple illustrations may be given.

Mark 1[14f.] gives in summary form an account of what
Jesus proclaimed: The time is up; the kingdom of God
has come near; repent, and believe in this good news.
This is bare proclamation, a naked word, not specifically
related (except by implication) to the person of the
speaker, and not attached to any particular event. Much
later (in 6[1-6]) Mark recounts a visit of Jesus to His native
place. Alike in healing and in preaching the visit is unsuccessful; there are few cures, and Jesus' fellow-citizens
are unwilling to believe that one whose family they know
so well can be less insignificant than themselves. These
two pieces of Marcan material are combined by Luke,
with other material, in a highly dramatic incident (4[16-30]),
which anticipates the course of the ministry. A few words
suffice[68] to bring before the reader a representative Jewish
congregation gathered to hear the reading of the Old
Testament. Jesus asserts that the prophetic lection is fulfilled *in him*—for his words 'This day is this Scripture
fulfilled in your ears' can mean nothing less than this.

[67] See p. 48, n. 47.
[68] It is characteristic of Luke's artistry that he excels as a miniaturist.
His larger canvases lack coherence, but the details are vivid.

The story goes on to depict (1) the immediate acceptance of the gracious words of Jesus by all fair-minded hearers; (2) the prediction of the Gentile mission; (3) the wrath of the Jews and their rejection of Jesus; (4) His miraculous deliverance from death. All this takes place within a page of biographical writing, and it represents the pattern of the divine purpose which was expressed in the life of Jesus as a whole.

Luke's handling of the apocalyptic material is even more striking. His most notable modification of the Marcan apocalypse[69] is the replacement of Mark's prediction that the abomination of desolation will stand 'where he ought not' by an oracle describing Jerusalem surrounded by army camps, with evident reference to the siege and destruction of the city by the Romans (Mark 13[14]; Luke 21[20]). Whether Luke made up this oracle on the basis of Old Testament patterns, or took it over from some non-Marcan source[70] is a disputed question that need not be discussed here; it is simple fact that he has substituted for the most mysteriously apocalyptic element in Mark a straightforward reference to a historical event. Luke retains the conviction that the Son of man is to come in glory at some future time, but his eye fastens on the notorious historical events of A.D. 70 as the best means of demonstrating God's activity, and the certainty of the hope which he and his readers shared.

It is only superficially that the apocalypse of Luke 17

[69] This sentence implies the view that Luke 21 is an edited version of Mark 13, a view I should be prepared to defend in detail if space permitted.

[70] For the linguistic parallels between the Lucan oracle and the Greek Old Testament, see C. H. Dodd, 'The Fall of Jerusalem and the "Abomination of Desolation"', *Journal of Roman Studies,* xxxvii (1947), pp. 47-54. Dodd's conclusion is that 'of the alternative forms of oracle the Lucan is consistent and readily intelligible from well-known passages of the Old Testament, while the Marcan shows signs of composition from dispersed material and remains obscure'. (Reprinted in the second volume of Dodd's collected essays, *More New Testament Studies* [Grand Rapids, 1968], pp. 69-83.)

appears to contradict this view. In 17²⁰ᶠ· it is denied
that there will be premonitory signs[71] of the coming of
the kingdom of God, but here Luke is speaking of the
End itself. Before this, there will be an interval in which
history proceeds, and it is in this period that from time
to time observable signs will show that God is watching
over His word to perform it. The interval will not be
short. Mark 13⁶ contains a warning against those de-
ceivers who declare: 'I am he' (ἐγώ εἰμι); Luke retains
this warning, but adds another, against those who say
'The time is near' (ὁ καιρὸς ἤγγικεν). There will be a
period sufficient for a significant amount of Church History; compare also Luke 19¹¹. The programme is made
more explicit in Acts 1⁷ᶠ·: the time of the End is an
unrevealed secret; what is revealed is that under the
inspiration of the Spirit the Church is to spread the
Gospel to the end of the earth. Acts simply follows out
this pattern of activity.

Luke's representation of the divine plan of redemptive
history has been hinted at above. Dr Conzelmann is
right in saying that Luke depicts Jesus as the 'middle of
time', though it must not be forgotten that Luke insists
as strongly as any New Testament writer on the second
coming of Christ. This is Luke's answer to the problem
of time. He contributes further to the solution of the
eschatological problem at the end of the first century by
asserting, and, as far as he can, demonstrating, the essential unity in faith and proclamation between the Church
of his own age, and that of the first days after the ascension.

[71] The most recent discussion of these verses is by A. Rüstow, in *Zeitschrift für die neutestamentliche Wissenschaft*, li (1960), pp. 197-224. He summarizes his interpretation of Luke 17²⁰ᵇ on p. 203: 'Das Gottesreich kommt
nicht unter Vorausberechnung, nicht so, dass der Zeitpunkt seines Kommens
vorausberechnet werden könnte, es kommt nicht in vorausberechenbarer
Weise.'

Luke is a practical writer. The whole of his two-volume work is rightly described as preaching. It sets forth Jesus Christ, crucified and risen, as the one means of salvation. 'In no other is there salvation; nor is there any other name under heaven, which is given among men, by which we must be saved' (Acts 4¹²). The gospel is the story of the Saviour himself; Acts contains sermons which set him forth, and stories which illustrate the power of the preaching. There are in addition several specific lessons which Luke seems anxious to teach.

(1) The Church now, in this world, lives under the rule of Jesus Christ the Lord, who works through the Spirit. It seems better to express the matter in this way than in terms of the Spirit only,⁷² for not only is the Lord said to have poured forth the Spirit (Acts 2³³), He is Himself directly operative in the work of His people, so that the heavenly voice can say to Saul, 'Why persecutest thou me?' (9⁴). It is everywhere assumed that it is the duty of Christian men to obey the orders of their Lord (e.g. 9¹⁰⁻¹⁷); and equally it is assumed that the Lord will not leave His people without the direction and support that they need (e.g. 18⁹ff·). It is true, however, that the usual agent of admonition and comfort is the Spirit. Luke's conception of the Trinity can scarcely be said to have achieved fully orthodox shape: the Father sends the Son, and the Son sends the Spirit, a somewhat hierarchical view of the Trinity being implied; but (and this is the decisive point for Trinitarian theology) the operations of the Spirit never bear any valuation lower than the operation of God. He too is the Lord, in that when He commands men must obey (e.g. 10¹⁹ff·). It is characteristic of Acts, and it is important, that the activities of the Spirit are most often directed outwards; that is, they do less to build up an inward, 'spiritual' life than

---

⁷² Cf. Ehrhardt's view, as summarized above on pp. 35f.

to convey the Gospel to new fields, and this both in prompting and directing evangelism (e.g. 8²⁹; 16⁶ᶠ·), and in equipping the evangelists (e.g. 4⁸; 6⁵; 13⁹). This suggests a further point on which Luke lays great stress.

(2) The prime agency by which the Spirit extends the sovereignty of Christ is the Word of God,[73] the testimony to Jesus Christ. Luke describes the work of apostles and evangelists as speaking, or proclaiming, or 'evangelizing' ($\epsilon\vec{v}\alpha\gamma\gamma\epsilon\lambda\acute{\iota}\zeta\epsilon\sigma\theta\alpha\iota$) the Word; those who hear it and believe are said to accept or receive the Word. When the affairs of the Church are prospering he says that the Word grows and multiplies. He mentions this speaking, accepting, and multiplying of the Word thirty-two times. The expression is used also at 6², ⁴ to describe an activity to which the apostles in particular must devote themselves; to this corresponds the appointment of the Twelve as special witnesses (1⁸; *et al.*); the Word of God is testimony to Jesus, and especially to His resurrection (4³³). But the preaching of the Word and the proclamation of Jesus are by no means confined to the apostles, or to any official group (e.g. 8⁴; 11¹⁹).[74] It would be absurd to describe Acts as anti-sacramental, for Luke speaks of baptism as the normal means by which converted men enter the Church, and of a 'breaking of bread'; but in Acts it is beyond question the preaching of the Word by which the Church lives and grows. This conviction leads to a third special intention in Luke's writing.

(3) One cannot doubt that Luke wrote as he did, and what he did, because he believed it to be vital that the Church of his own time should recall and adhere to the

[73] I include here several expressions: $\acute{o}$ $\lambda\acute{o}\gamma os$ $\tauo\hat{v}$ $\theta\epsilon o\hat{v}$ ($\sigmao v$); $\acute{o}$ $\lambda\acute{o}\gamma os$ $\tauo\hat{v}$ $\kappa v\rho\acute{\iota}o v$; $\acute{o}$ $\lambda\acute{o}\gamma os$ $\tau\hat{\eta}s$ $\sigma\omega\tau\eta\rho\acute{\iota}\alpha s$; $\acute{o}$ $\lambda\acute{o}\gamma os$ $\tauo\hat{v}$ $\epsilon\vec{v}\alpha\gamma\gamma\epsilon\lambda\acute{\iota}o v$; also $\acute{o}$ $\lambda\acute{o}\gamma os$ *simpliciter*.

[74] Note also the existence of Christians in places such as Damascus, Lydda, and Joppa, where we do not know who first preached.

preaching of the apostolic age.[75] Only so can one account for his repetition of speeches cast in substantially the same terms.[76] Even if every speech or sermon were a literally accurate account of what was said on each occasion it would not be necessary for the historian so to repeat himself, unless he wished to hammer home the truth: This is how Peter preached; this is how Paul preached; this is how Christians ought always to preach. There is perhaps another point here in the relation between Luke-Acts and the Pastoral Epistles.[77] In the Pastorals, the minister is enjoined to preach the Word constantly, in season and out of season. Acts not only sets a good example of this unwearied evangelism, but also provides the preacher with models on which his own preaching may be based. He cannot do better than proclaim the Gospel as Peter and Paul proclaimed it. Further, their deeds as well as their words are exemplary for the minister, and Paul's farewell address to the Ephesian elders (Acts 20[18-35]) is a piece of pastoral advice and encouragement which Luke, we may suppose, intended his fellow-ministers to take to heart.

(4) Luke thus has a special word for the Church's ministry in his own day; but he also depicts a pattern of Christian life that applies to all believers. Man is a sinner, and the only way for him to enter upon life with God is forgiveness (e.g. Luke 7[48]; Acts 2[38]); this is possible through the free mercy of God, which appeared in the gracious dealing of Jesus with all those whom the

[75] This observation has a negative corollary which will be mentioned below (pp. 72ff.). It is important to know, and to reproduce, the doctrine the apostles taught, and the life they lived; no other mode of connection with the apostles seems important.

[76] See the classical exposition of the common material in the speeches by C. H. Dodd in *The Apostolic Preaching and its Developments* (London, first edition 1936). The many subsequent analyses do not add substantially to the fundamental observation that most of the speeches show the same pattern.

[77] See p. 63.

rest of men despised—sinners (e.g. Luke 15²), tax-
collectors (e.g. Luke 19¹), Samaritans (e.g. Luke 17¹⁶),
Gentiles (e.g. Luke 7⁹), and women (e.g. Luke 7³⁷)—
and then became permanently available through the
Gospel preached by the apostles and their colleagues
(e.g. Luke 24⁴⁷; Acts 13³⁸). The fruit of forgiveness is
the life of obedience in love (e.g. Luke 6³⁶; 7⁴⁷; Acts 7⁶⁰;
11²⁹). Forgiveness and obedience are both of them sealed
in baptism by the gift of the Spirit (e.g. Acts 2³⁸; 19⁵ᶠ·;
but cf. also such passages as 13⁴⁸, ⁵², where there is no
reference to baptism); and Christians appear to have
held a common meal, though little stress is laid on the
fact (Acts 2⁴², ⁴⁶; 20⁷⁻¹²). This pattern of Christian life
is in fact Paulinism, though at a lower pitch. Luke uses
the Pauline verb 'to justify' (Luke 10²⁹; 16¹⁵; 18¹⁴; Acts
13³⁹), though it may be questioned whether he has fully
understood its theological depth. Luke is no Paul, but
he is a Paulinist,⁷⁸ doing his best to make available to
a new age the doctrines of the apostle he admired. And
though he reaches neither the depths nor the heights of
his master—failing, for example, to see the point of the
controversy about the Gentile mission—there is no reason
to think that he would have been disowned by him.

This claim will bring us to the last question we shall
discuss. Is it 'primitive catholicism' (*Frühkatholizismus*)⁷⁹
that we encounter in the Lucan writings, or not? If
Frühkatholizismus is taken as the designation of a Church
aware of the problems of gnosticism and of eschatology,
defending itself against gnostic corruption and redefining
its eschatology in view of the lengthening period between
the resurrection and the *parousia*, the answer must be yes.
But if *Frühkatholizismus* means more than this; if it means

---

⁷⁸ That is, an admirer of Paul; one who takes his part, and reproduces
his doctrinal system, not perfectly, but as well as he is able.
⁷⁹ See p. 25.

that the Church is now viewed as a *Heilsanstalt*, an insti-
tution dispensing salvation; if it means that 'the Word
is no longer the single criterion of the Church, but the
Church legitimizes the Word, and the apostolic origin of
ecclesiastical office affords the guarantee for legitimate
preaching';[80] if it means that Luke's is a theology which
differs essentially from that of primitive Christianity;
then we shall hesitate before making the same reply.

That there are occasional passages which may be taken
to point in the direction of *Frühkatholizismus* is perhaps
true; such a passage is Acts 19^{1-7}, where the disciples of
John the Baptist are brought into the Spirit-filled Church
by baptism and the imposition of hands.[81] It would,
however, be mistaken to base a general conclusion on
a few incidents; and when Luke-Acts is considered as a
whole a different picture results. Some of the most
important points are the following.

For Luke, the apostles are essentially witnesses; in
particular they are witnesses of the resurrection (Luke
24^{48}; Acts 1^{22}; 4^{33}; $10^{40f.}$). This role lays upon them
the task of preaching, and Luke represents them as de-
voted to the ministry of the Word ($6^{2, 4}$). They are not,
in his view, administrators. It is implied by 2^{42} and
other passages that they also taught; but in Luke's usage
teaching is almost identical with preaching (e.g. Acts
$5^{25, 28}$; 13^{12}; 18^{11}). The silent disappearance of the
Twelve from Luke's narrative (they are mentioned under
this name only at 6^2 (cf. 1^{26}; 2^{14}); as 'the apostles' they
last appear in a reference to the so-called Council in
16^4) shows both that he had little knowledge about them
apart from their number (he knows that James was
murdered, and that Peter went to 'another place'), and

---

[80] The quotation is taken from p. 21 of Käsemann's article referred to
on p. 25, n. 28. Most of the points in the surrounding lines are drawn
from the same paragraph (pp. 20f.). (*Ex. Ver. II,* pp. 29f.; Eng. trans.,
pp. 21f.)

[81] For the significance of Acts 8^{14}; 11^{22}, see the next note.

also that he had no intention of magnifying them into
religious dictators. Their unique place in the Church
was secured not by their personality or office, but by
their testimony. Further, they were not the only evangelists. The Christians dispersed at the time of the persecution which arose over Stephen acted not merely as
assistants in the work of evangelism but as its spearhead;
they, for example, first preached to non-Jews in Antioch.[82]
Barnabas, Silas, Timothy, and others take second place
in relation to Paul, but no explanation of this is needed
beyond Luke's hero-worship and the sheer facts of the
matter. It is evident from the epistles that there could
be only one leader in the Pauline circle; but the same
epistles make it as clear as does Acts that Paul's colleagues
were like himself preachers, pastors, and evangelists.
Luke's stress on the proclamation of the Word, which we
have already noted, shows that the Word itself was the
decisive factor. It was by the Word that Luke rebutted
gnosticism.

Consideration of the apostles and their assistants leads
to the ministry. There is nothing in his treatment of
this subject to suggest that Luke had any ecclesiastical
axe to grind. Elders are mentioned (Acts 11[30]; 14[23];
15[2, 4, 6, 22, 23]; 16[4]; 20[17]; 21[18]), and once the term

---

[82] It is true that in Acts 11[22] the Jerusalem church (*not* the apostles) are
said to hear of this development and to send Barnabas on a mission of, it
may be, inspection, or of confirmation. This might be taken to suggest
the importance of direct ecclesiastical contact with the original body of
disciples. Haenchen (*ad. loc.*) has shown, however, that Acts 11[19-26] is
a Lucan construction, and that the 'inspection' (if that is what is intended)
is introduced not on ecclesiastical but on literary grounds, since Barnabas
was involved, and Luke had already (4[36f.]) represented him as connected
with the apostles. Acts 8[14] can be similarly explained; but in each case
even more important than literary considerations is the fact that it is vital
to Luke's purpose (see pp. 57f.; also pp. 49 and 6of.) to show that the whole
Christian mission sprang from the work of Jesus, and that he does this by
introducing a connection between each missionary development and the
Jerusalem church. It is a historical not an ecclesiastical device that he
employs, and he is not thinking in terms of apostolic authorization.

'bishop' appears as synonymous with elder (20²⁸); deacons are never mentioned at all.⁸³ We cannot safely infer from Acts the existence of more than one 'order' of ministers.⁸⁴ How the elders in Jerusalem came into being we are not informed; there is not the least hint of any transfer of authority from the apostles.⁸⁵ The statement in 14²³ that Paul and Barnabas appointed (χειροτονεῖν) elders is not consistent with the Pauline epistles, which never mention elders; here Luke has probably described in the terms of his own day the far less formal way in which in the Pauline churches certain persons came to be marked out as leaders;⁸⁶ but Acts 20²⁸ shows that Luke, like Paul, knew where the true appointment lay: it is not men, even apostles, but the Holy Spirit who makes ministers in the Church. Of all New Testament books, the Acts of the Apostles is that which might most naturally have been expected to indicate that succession from the apostles was a necessary condition of the Church's ministry; but of such a succession there is not a whisper.⁸⁷ Luke was satisfied that the apostles and their friends were good men who did preach true doctrine, but he lends no support to the view that they did so because of some apostolic mystique (apart from their qualification as eye-witnesses of the ministry and resurrection of Jesus)

⁸³ It should not be necessary to point out that the Seven (Acts 6) are not described as deacons. The language of Acts 6², ⁴ is strongly against Luke's having thought of them as διάκονοι.

⁸⁴ Though there is a variety of ministers (or ministries) in Acts: prophets, evangelists, teachers, and so forth. The word 'order' is an anachronism as far as Acts is concerned.

⁸⁵ Not even if (without evidence) we regard the Seven as elders.

⁸⁶ Paul never refers to πρεσβύτεροι. Apart from the isolated reference in Phil. 1¹ to ἐπίσκοποι and διάκονοι, the Pauline letters speak in an informal way of persons who 'take the lead' or 'preside': Rom. 12⁸ (ὁ προϊστάμενος); 1 Cor. 12²⁸ (ἀντιλήμψεις, κυβερνήσεις); 16¹⁵⁻¹⁸ (note ἔταξαν ἑαυτούς); 1 Thess. 5¹² (τοὺς κοπιῶντας . . . καὶ προϊσταμένους . . . καὶ νουθετοῦντας). Leadership existed, though in no marked degree; but it was not formulated as eldership.

⁸⁷ Cf. Conzelmann as summarized on p. 45, Haenchen on p. 47.

which guaranteed their status and orthodoxy and could
be transmitted along an orderly line of succession—their
character as eye-witnesses naturally could not be transmitted at all. His picture is a happier one than the facts
warrant,[88] but the spectacles through which he sees it
are rose-tinted with hero-worship, not distorted by
ecclesiastical prejudice.

To Luke, the Church (ἡ ἐκκλησία) is almost always the
local church.[89] It is the theme of his work that the outcome of the life and death of Jesus was a community
which expanded from Jerusalem to fill the world, but
he sees clearly that this world-wide body was made up
of local groups, and expanded through the multiplica-
tion of local groups, which, though they maintained the
links of charity and brotherhood and were united by a
common faith, were each of them in a proper sense
churches. At first, the mother-church at Jerusalem exercises a natural presidency; but Luke makes no attempt
to whitewash it for its coldness towards the great apostle
at the time of his arrest and imprisonment, and after
the Council (Acts 15) it is scarcely even the centre of
missionary operations. The Church is more than an
aggregation of all local churches, but this does not in
itself make it a *Heilsanstalt*. Such an agency of salvation
it is only in so far as it provides the framework within
which the preaching of the Word takes place, and thus
in its totality and local particularity bears witness to the
fact of Christ. Luke does not believe in the existence of
salvation or of Christians outside the Church, but this is

[88] Note especially the absence of controversy between the leaders. Gal. 2
gives a different impression.

[89] Cf. Haenchen's observation, given on p. 47. This is correct. At Acts
9[31], many MSS. read the plural αἱ ἐκκλησίαι, with corresponding verbs
and participles. This reading is probably incorrect, but even so the verse
scarcely forms an exception, since in it the dimensions of the church are
strictly limited (καθ' ὅλης τῆς Ἰουδαίας καὶ Γαλιλαίας καὶ Σαμαρείας); it
is in fact a local church on a large scale.

because he knows that it is in the context of the Church that the saving Word must be heard and believed, and because it does not occur to him that any sincere believer would wish to separate himself from those to whom he owed it. He emphasizes the fact that the divine plan is always thrusting outwards, and works a step ahead of the organized community. The Spirit falls on Cornelius and his associates before their baptism (Acts 10^{44}), and Apollos is already burning in Spirit (18^{25}) before he receives official instruction. Apollos, though he knew only the baptism of John, was not rebaptized; a group of John's disciples mentioned in the next chapter were rebaptized (19^5). In view of facts such as these it can scarcely be maintained that Luke's view of the sacraments represents the Church as purveying salvation along official sacramental channels. So far is he from setting forth an orderly and 'official' view of the sacraments that it is notoriously impossible[90] to reconstruct a harmonious account of what he believed about baptism, and his allusions to the eucharist (if such indeed they are) are as slight and informal as they could be. He is less interested in, and less profound in his treatment of, the sacraments than Paul. He sees the Church not as a hierarchical *Heilsanstalt* but as a loosely-knit evangelistic and pastoral organism.

Little would be gained by contending about names, such as 'primitive catholicism' and (as a possible alternative) 'developed paulinism', for these can mean as little or as much as we please. It would be more instructive, as a last step in our discussion, to compare Luke-Acts with contemporary documents[91] which cannot be

[90] See pp. 23, 68, 70, 71.

[91] 1 Clement is commonly dated *c.* A.D. 95; the letters of Ignatius about twenty years later. There is no early evidence for the existence of Luke-Acts, and the most probable view is that it was written in or near this period.

denied the title of *Frühkatholizismus*, such as the epistles of Clement and Ignatius. Here too we see the Church protecting itself against gnosticism and giving itself a new orientation in regard to eschatology; but the means adopted differ *toto caelo* from Luke's. They are ecclesiastical, ministerial, authoritarian, and sacramental, whereas Luke contents himself with the historical task of reconstructing the story of Jesus, and of depicting the life, thought, and preaching of the earliest days of Christianity. For him, the Church of later days will be apostolic not in virtue of a succession or pattern of ministry, but by doing and teaching what the apostles did and taught. It would be a profitable task to imagine what the Gospel and Acts would have looked like if Clement or Ignatius had written them.

I have no space here in which to pursue this exercise of the imagination; but as I contemplate it I give thanks for the divine providence which made the New Testament Canon what it is, and thereby made authoritative Luke's picture of the apostolic Church which lives by and for the Word, rather than the Clementine and Ignatian deviations from this norm. It is at this point that it becomes clear in how limited a sense we may speak of Luke as a 'vehicle of the spirit of the age' (p. 53, above). It was another Spirit that enabled him to address to his age a message differing far more sharply than might have been expected from current Christian opinion as this is revealed to us outside the New Testament.

Select Bibliography since 1960

(I am indebted to Mr. S. G. Wilson, of Durham, who has prepared the material for this bibliography. I regret that limitations of space forbid the presentation of the much longer list of titles that he has collected.—CKB)

1. For Reference. The following are indispensable:

MATTILL, A. J., JR., and M. B. *A Classified Bibliography of Literature on the Acts of the Apostles.* ("New Testament Tools and Studies," 7.) Leiden: Brill, 1966.

GRÄSSER, E. "Die Apostelgeschichte in der Forschung der Gegenwart," *Theologische Rundschau,* N.F. 26 (1960), 93–167. A definitive research report; the next four are more brief.

WILLIAMS, C. S. C. "Luke-Acts in Recent Study," *Expository Times,* 73 (1961–62), 133–36.

MARSHALL, I. H. "Recent Study of the Gospel according to St. Luke," *Expository Times,* 80 (1968–69), 4–8.

ROHDE, JOACHIM. *Rediscovering the Teaching of the Evangelists.* ("The New Testament Library.") Trans. Dorothea M. Barton, London: SCM, 1968. Pp. 153–239 summarize, often with a brief critique, the views of Conzelmann, W. Grundmann's commentary (Berlin, 1961), Lohse, Luck, Bartsch, Vielhauer, Haenchen, Wilckens, Rese, Klein, Flender, and Robinson (listed below) on the Gospel of Luke.

2. Commentaries. The following list does not include new editions of those previously published.

On Luke:

CAIRD, GEORGE B. *The Gospel of St. Luke.* ("Pelican Gospel Commentaries.") Harmondsworth, 1963. New York: Seabury, 1968.

ELLIS, E. EARLE. *The Gospel of Luke.* ("The Century Bible, New Edition [Based on the R.S.V.].") London: Nelson, 1966.

On Acts:

CONZELMANN, HANS. *Die Apostelgeschichte.* ("Handbuch zum Neuen Testament," 7.) Tübingen: J. C. B. Mohr (Paul Siebeck), 1963.

HANSON, R. P. C. *The Acts in the Revised Standard Version.* ("The New Clarendon Bible.") New York: Oxford University Press, 1967.

STÄHLIN, GUSTAV. *Die Apostelgeschichte.* ("Das Neue Testament Deutsch," 5.) Göttingen: Vandenhoeck & Ruprecht, 1962.

3. Important Studies. The following are among the most significant. For the many important articles, and other works, not included here, see the references given by authors named here and by Haenchen in the latest (1965) edition of his commentary.

BARTSCH, HANS-WERNER. *Wachet aber zu jeder Zeit! Entwurf einer Auslegung des Lukasevangeliums.* Hamburg-Bergstedt: Reich, 1963.

BETZ, OTTO. "The Kerygma of Luke," *Interpretation*, 22 (1968), 131–46.

BROWN, SCHUYLER, S. J. *Apostasy and Perseverance in the Theology of Luke*. ("Analecta Biblica," 36.) Rome: Pontifical Biblical Institute, 1969.

DUPONT, JACQUES, O.S.B. *The Sources of the Acts*. Trans. K. Pond. New York: Herder & Herder, 1964.

————. *Etudes sur les Actes des Apôtres*. ("Lectio Divina," 45.) Paris: Cerf, 1967. This is a collection of studies published at various times, and including a valuable account of work on Acts between 1940 and 1950.

FILSON, FLOYD V. *Three Crucial Decades: Studies in the Book of Acts*. Richmond: John Knox, 1963. Acts gives us a "generally dependable guide" to life in the early church.

FLENDER, HELMUT. *Saint Luke: Theologian of Redemptive History*. Trans. Reginald H. and I. Fuller. Philadelphia: Fortress, 1967. A study of the relation between history and theology in the Lucan writings; useful, though open to the charge of oversystematizing Luke.

HOLTZ, TRAUGOTT. *Untersuchungen über die alttestamentlichen Zitate bei Lukas*. ("Texte und Untersuchungen," 104.) Berlin: Akademie Verlag, 1968.

KECK, LEANDER, and MARTYN, J. L., eds. *Studies in Luke-Acts: Essays Presented in Honor of Paul Schubert*. New York: Abingdon, 1966. London, 1968. A very valuable collection of essays on many important themes, giving a comprehensive panorama of modern work on Luke-Acts. Of the previously unpublished articles, those of Bornkamm, Conzelmann, Dahl, Fitzmyer, Haenchen, and Wilckens are particularly important.

KLEIN, GÜNTHER. *Die zwölf Apostel—Ursprung und Gehalt einer Idee*. ("Forschung zur Religion und Literatur des Alten und Neuen Testamentes," N.F. 59.) Göttingen: Vandenhoeck & Ruprecht, 1961. Klein's main thesis is that Luke both gave and limited the title *apostle* to the Twelve. Luke's motive was to reclaim Paul for the church from gnostics who were claiming him as their own authority; he does this by denying Paul apostolic status and portraying him as subordinate to and dependent on the Twelve. Klein thinks that Luke deliberately wrote a perverted account of Paul though he was aware of the facts from the epistles. He carefully analyzes large sections of Acts, and the chief value of his book is that it forces the reader to do likewise. For a critique, see W. Schmithals, *Das kirchliche Apostelamt. Eine historische Untersuchung* (["Forschung zur Religion und Literatur des Alten und Neuen Testamentes," N.F., 61]

Göttingen, 1961); Eng. trans. by J. E. Steely, *The Office of Apostle in the Early Church* (New York: Abingdon, 1969).

———. "Lukas 1, 1–4 als theologisches Programm," in *Zeit und Geschichte: Dankesgabe an R. Bultmann zum 80. Geburtstag.* Tübingen: J. C. B. Mohr [Paul Siebeck], 1964. Pp. 193–216.

LOHSE, EDUARD. "Lukas als Theologe der Heilsgeschichte," *Evangelische Theologie,* 14 (1954), 256–75.

O'NEILL, J. C. *The Theology of Acts in Its Historical Setting.* London: S.P.C.K., 1961. O'Neill dates Acts between A.D. 115 and 130, mainly on the basis of its Christology and affinities with second-century writers, especially Justin. He then discusses various other themes in Acts, concluding that Acts is primarily an apology, designed to persuade educated Romans to become Christians, and that it shows affinities with other Hellenistic-Jewish missionary literature. Subsidiary purposes are to show (a) that the whole Christian movement has been under God's guidance, (b) the disengagement of Christianity from Judaism to become a distinct entity, and the political innocence of Christianity. Luke incidentally addressed the church on the topics of false apocalypticism, church unity, and the church's future in the gentile world. In his comparisons with other early Christian literature O'Neill has made a start in a neglected field, but much remains to be done. For critiques see Hans Conzelmann in *Studies in Luke-Acts* (above), pp. 302 ff., and the review by H. F. D. Sparks in *Journal of Theological Studies,* n.s. 14 (1963), 457–66.

OTT, W. *Gebet und Heil. Die Bedeutung der Gebetsparänese in der lukanischen Theologie.* ("Studien zum Alten und Neuen Testament," 12.) Munich: Kösel-Verlag, 1965.

RESE, M. *Alttestamentliche Motive in der Christologie des Lukas.* Bonn, 1965.

ROBINSON, W. C., JR. *Der Weg des Herrn. Studien zur Geschichte und Eschatologie im Lukas-Evangelium. Ein Gespräch mit H. Conzelmann.* ("Theologische Forschung," 36.) Hamburg-Bergstedt: Reich, 1964. This aims at being partly a critique of Conzelmann's *Theology of St Luke,* and partly a new exposition of Lucan theology. It is generally more successful in the former aim than in the latter. A useful corrective for Conzelmann.

———. "The Theological Context for Interpreting Luke's Travel Narrative (9:51 ff.)," *Journal of Biblical Literature,* 79 (1960), 20–31.

SCHMITHALS, WALTER. *Paul and James.* ("Studies in Biblical Theology," 46.) London: SCM, 1965.

SCHULZ, SIEGFRIED. *Die Stunde der Botschaft. Einführung in die Theologie der vier Evangelisten.* Hamburg: Furche-Verlag, 1967.

TALBERT, CHARLES HAROLD. *Luke and the Gnostics: An Examination of the Lucan Purpose.* New York: Abingdon, 1966. Talbert presents the thesis that Luke-Acts was written as a defense against gnosticism. He sees the following themes as antignostic devices: "authentic witness" which guarantees the church's proclamation; the appeal to apostolic authority as a guarantee for the church's exegesis of the Old Testament; the belief in a "succession of tradition" (Acts 18,20); the significance of martyrdom. The lack of direct reference to gnosticism in Luke-Acts is a result of Luke's idealization of the apostolic era, which is a further attack on gnosticism, since it implies that heresy was a postapostolic phenomenon. The book attempts to explore a neglected area in Lucan studies, but raises more questions than it answers.

————. "An Anti-Gnostic Tendency in Lucan Christology," *New Testament Studies,* 14 (1967–68), 259–71.

VIELHAUER, PHILIPP. "On the 'Paulinism' of Acts," originally in *Evangelische Theologie,* 10 (1950–51), 1–15; Eng. trans. reprinted in *Studies in Luke-Acts* (above), pp. 33–50. cf. E. Käsemann, "Paulus und der Frühkatholizismus," *ZThK,* 60 (1963), 75–89, reprinted in *Ex. Ver. II* (above, p. 25, n. 28), pp. 239–52; Eng. trans. (see above, p. 25, n. 28), pp. 236–51; and contrast P. Borgen, "Von Paulus zu Lukas. Beobachtungen zur Erhellung der Theologie der Lukasschriften," *Studia Theologica,* 20 (1966), 140–57.

VOSS, G., O.S.B. *Die Christologie der lukanischen Schriften in Grundzügen.* ("Studia Neotestamentica, Studia," 2). Bruges: Desclée de Brouwer, 1965.

WILCKENS, U. *Die Missionsreden der Apostelgeschichte. Form- und traditionsgeschichtliche Untersuchungen.* ("Wissenschaftliche Monographien zum Alten und Neuen Testament," 5.) 2d ed. Neukirchen, 1963. A detailed analysis of the context, structure, and content of the speeches in Acts, following the work of Dodd and Dibelius. Wilckens concludes that they are creations of Luke and therefore represent the theology of Luke and of the church at the end of the first century, and not the theology of the primitive church. The concluding chapter contains a useful discussion of the main views on Luke's theology. Wilckens thinks that Luke's weakness is not, as Käsemann and Conzelmann think, his *heilsgeschichtlich* scheme but his lack of a serious *theologia crucis.* For a short critique see E. Haenchen's commentary (above, p. 46, n. 44), p. 680. Eng. trans. announced.

WILCOX, MAX. *The Semitisms of Acts.* New York: Oxford University Press, 1965.